Country
of the
Heart

Mak Mak (The white-breasted sea-eagle) waiting for a feed.

Country
of the
Heart

An Indigenous Australian Homeland

Deborah Bird Rose with Nancy Daiyi, Kathy Deveraux,
Margaret Daiyi, Linda Ford and April Bright

Photographs by Sharon D'Amico

 Aboriginal
Studies
Press

First published in 2002
by Aboriginal Studies Press

Second edition published in 2011 by Aboriginal Studies Press

Aboriginal Studies Press
is the publishing arm of the
Australian Institute of Aboriginal
and Torres Strait Islander Studies.
GPO Box 553, Canberra, ACT 2601
Phone: (61 2) 6246 1183
Fax: (61 2) 6261 4288
Email: asp@aiatsis.gov.au
Web: www.aiatsis.gov.au/asp/about.html

National Library of Australia Cataloguing-in-Publication entry

Author: Rose, Deborah Bird, 1946-

Title: Country of the heart: an Australian indigenous homeland/ Deborah Bird Rose, Sharon D'Amico.

Edition: 2nd ed.

ISBN: 9780855757762 (pbk.)

Notes: Includes index.

Subjects: Aboriginal Australians — Northern Territory — Wagait Region. Women, Aboriginal Australian — Northern Territory — Wagait Region. Wagait Region (N.T.)

Other Authors/Contributors:
D'Amico, Sharon.

Dewey Number: 305.89915

Edited by Theresa Willsteed
Design and typesetting by Rachel Ippoliti, Aboriginal Studies Press

Printed in China by Phoenix Offset Pty Ltd

Cover: Nancy Daiyi at Didjini

CONTENTS

A NOTE ON ORTHOGRAPHY

Inconsistencies of spelling seem to me to be a good reminder that these languages are first and foremost oral languages, not written ones. Like the stories that often twist and turn in the telling, so too does spelling twist and turn in the writing.

Kathy Deveraux has been a student of linguistics at Batchelor Community College, and is working on an orthography for the Mak Mak Marranunggu (Marra Warrgat) language. In this book I have retained place name spellings as they have been presented in other texts. Following are some guidelines to pronunciation for readers:

- 'ty' is pronounced like 'j' in 'jewel' (or 'dual', in Australian English);

- 'rr' sounds like 'd', as in 'madder';

- the use of 'y' after 'n' gives a stronger 'n' sound, but is itself not pronounced. Thus, 'Bulkany' would be written phonetically as 'Bulkine'.

Warning: The toxic plants discussed in this book may contain lethal levels of toxins and should not be handled or eaten except under the personal direction of knowledgeable teachers.

Aboriginal and Torres Strait Islander people are respectfully advised that this publication contains names and images of deceased persons.

PREFACE

I came to the floodplains after having studied for thirteen years with Aboriginal people in the semi-arid savannas of North Australia. I was staggered by the richness and variety of the country. Everything seemed exaggerated: the king tides came rolling in across the dry land, the crocodiles were huge 'man-eaters', the turtles dug themselves into the mud. On hot days, the dark peat soil radiated heat like an oven, and if a fire got started it would actually race along underground. The amount of food was astonishing. I became fascinated by the people who loved this country that, to me, seemed to be a decidedly unlovable swamp. I could see the beauty, but it took time to begin to empathise with the Indigenous people's love for their hot, humid, crocodile-infested homeland.

The clan of the white-breasted sea-eagle, or Mak Mak people (the White Eagle people), are also aware of discrepancies between their experience of country and that of strangers. A member of the clan, Kathy Deveraux, wrote:

Kathy: When strangers visit our country, we observe with a keen interest the way they respond and react to the panoramic view stretched out before them. What are they really seeing and thinking? We reckon they may be thinking about the beautiful scenery or just simply enjoying the peace and quiet or the wide-open spaces. Together we stand gazing at the same scenery. We look beyond the pristine beauty of the bush decked out in all its glory. The land contains our stories, it's enriching and powerful.[1]

After working together on the Wagait dispute (see pp. 97–99) — an experience that bonded us in our commitment to justice for the people and the entwined issue of environmental justice for the country — we began talking about a book. I had become interested in finding non-linear ways to communicate the structural and affective properties of a living system that keeps circling back on itself, and I thought a photo essay might offer alternatives. A photo essay could also show something of the plenitude and real world quality of life in an Indigenous homeland.

I met Sharon D'Amico, an American eco-photographer, and found a wonderfully empathetic quality in her work. In 1996, Sharon agreed to come to Australia to see if she and the Mak Mak people could work happily together. Sharon travelled all over Mak Mak country with clan members, creating

Deborah Bird Rose.

Sharon D'Amico. (Photo by Steve Fish)

photographs, observing, being taught, asking questions. On each of Sharon's two trips to Australia we hired a pilot and light aircraft, and flew low over the country with Linda Ford as our guide. The pilot took the door off the aeroplane so that Sharon could lean out and take photos. We took the slides back to the clan, and then held marathon slide shows and taped the discussions. Edited transcripts of these tapes provide most of the captions.

Almost all of the White Eagle people contributed to this book in one way or another, but the senior person, Nancy Daiyi, and her three daughters — Kathy Deveraux, Margaret Daiyi and Linda Ford — took on the majority of the tasks. The selection of photos to be included in the book was made jointly by Sharon, myself and the four Mak Mak women. In putting together the Mak Mak texts, I have drawn on published articles, taped discussions and transcripts of hearings before the Wagait committee. April Bright, Nancy's sister's daughter, is a wonderfully articulate senior woman. Unfortunately, April was unavailable during most of the research period for this book, but her presence is felt throughout.

Translations have been provided by Kathy Deveraux in consultation with the others. Marrithiel is the first language of these people, and Marranunggu and English are second languages. They all speak Aboriginal English and North Australian Kriol, and Nancy Daiyi speaks a number of other Indigenous languages as well. Kathy, Margaret, Linda, April and a few of the others also speak standard English. The linguistic register they use at any given moment is related to context, and in many of the slide discussions the audience included people who do not speak standard English. We have sought to retain the flavour of the original whilst ensuring that the texts will be accessible to people who do not know these languages.

The Mak Mak clan and associates. (Photo by D. Lewis)

Ngulilkang Nancy Daiyi (Photo by G. Deveraux)

TRIBUTE

Ngulilkang Nancy Daiyi was born in the bush in 1930's (exact year unknown). The youngest of a group of siblings, she lived her life in her home country, learning avidly from several generations of older bush people. She gave birth to four children, worked in the cattle industry, and throughout her whole life taught younger clans people the knowledge of country that was the essence of the relationships between the people and their homeland.

Some of the clan's most trying years arrived after her older siblings had passed away, leaving her as the last surviving member of her generation. She brought her years of learning together with her great strength of character to hold the group together as they struggled for legal recognition within Australian law. Throughout these years she drew on her awesome courage and determination to keep everyone focussed and committed.

Before she died, Ngulilkang Nancy Daiyi instructed her children to conduct a full–scale funeral in the old way. In 2007 she passed away and her body was formally placed on a platform at Kalngarriny, a central sacred site in the country (p. 85). Two years later the clan performed the second stage of the funeral, removing the remains of the body, and ensuring that all three song-styles of her country were performed. She thus joined her siblings and ancestors in the country they had loved and fought for.

Her great strength of character impressed everyone who knew her. She is remembered with both affection and awe, cherished for both her humour and her stern, unyielding commitments. A marvellous bush woman and a great hunter, she came from the country, and remains today a vivid presence in the on-going life of the country and the clan.

ACKNOWLEDGMENTS

From travelling across the country, to providing taped commentary, to working on translations and slide selections, proofreading and discussions, Mak Mak contributors have been patient and endlessly knowledgeable. Much of the work that went into this book was self-funded, as we were all committed to this project. In addition, we respectfully acknowledge the research funding we received from the Cooperative Research Centre for the Sustainable Development of Tropical Savannas, and the North Australia Research Unit, which is part of the Australian National University. This book was started while I was Senior Fellow in the Department of Anthropology, Research School of Pacific Studies, Australian National University, and was completed at the Centre for Resource and Environmental Studies, also at the Australian National University. These departments have provided equipment and collegiality, all of which is warmly appreciated.

Funding to assist publication has been generously provided by the Australian Academy of the Humanities and the Centre for Resource and Environmental Studies (ANU) and the ANU Publication Subsidy Committee.

This book owes its life to all of its contributors. The designer is special; she has the power to make or break the integrity of the holistic project. Rachel Ippoliti was faced with a design challenge that inspired her to present a multi-layered, textual, visual journey that continues to circle back on itself. Her unique talents brought the book to its full potential. Nona Cameron is an artist specialising in mapping sentient landscapes. Her innovative work in communicating the layers of dense and essential stories that are intrinsic to the country offers a pulsating iconic image of country. My gratitude to Rachel and Nona is without measure.

Deborah Bird Rose
Canberra, August 2002

MAP OF THE HOMELAND AREA

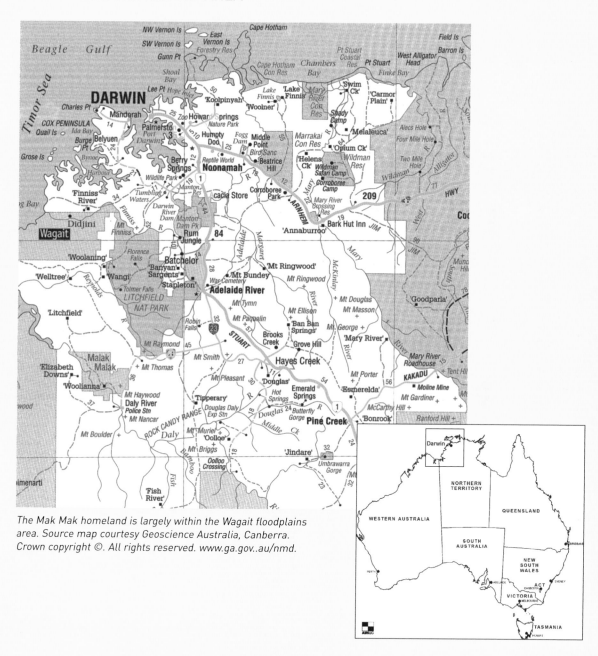

The Mak Mak homeland is largely within the Wagait floodplains area. Source map courtesy Geoscience Australia, Canberra. Crown copyright ©. All rights reserved. www.ga.gov..au/nmd.

GENEALOGICAL SKETCH

(For a full description of the clan's genealogy, see pp. 154–155)

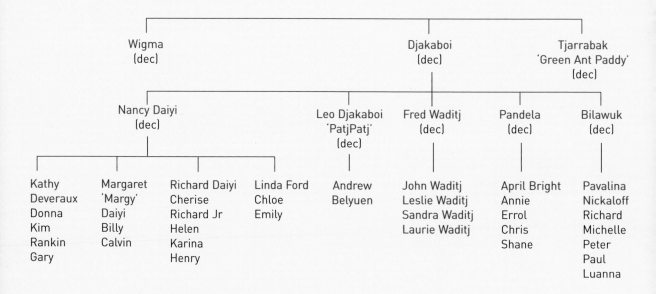

Wigma (dec)			Djakaboi (dec)		Tjarrabak 'Green Ant Paddy' (dec)
Nancy Daiyi (dec)			Leo Djakaboi 'PatjPatj' (dec)	Fred Waditj (dec)	Pandela (dec)	Bilawuk (dec)

Kathy Deveraux	Margaret 'Margy' Daiyi	Richard Daiyi	Linda Ford	Andrew Belyuen	John Waditj	April Bright	Pavalina Nickaloff
Donna	Billy	Cherise	Chloe		Leslie Waditj	Annie	Richard
Kim	Calvin	Richard Jr	Emily		Sandra Waditj	Errol	Michelle
Rankin		Helen			Laurie Waditj	Chris	Peter
Gary		Karina				Shane	Paul
		Henry					Luanna

MAP OF MAK MAK DREAMINGS

Illustration by Nona Cameron.

Mak Mak: The white-breasted sea-eagles.

Good Country

'My strength, the strength of the land. You can feel it in yourself, you belong there. It's your country, your dust, your place. You remember the old people. The white eagles always greet me. It's home. Safety and security. You see the birds, you see the country, and your senses come back to you. You know what to do and where to go.'

Mak Mak people

THE FLOODPLAINS

Fly to Darwin in the Northern Territory of Australia, and rent a four-wheel drive vehicle. Drive south-west to Litchfield National Park, going through the little bush town of Batchelor. As you near the park you leave the flat scrub of the Darwin hinterland and begin to climb the Tabletop Range. There comes a moment when you cross the watershed and catch a glimpse of the enormous western sky. Traces of smoke will tell you that there is land over there, and that the country is being 'fired'. The dense manner in which the light hangs in the air on the far horizon will tell you that the sea is there beyond. You feel transfixed, and yet nothing in these densities and opacities of light, air, water and fire tells you of the violence and love that are connected to this place.

You are seeing the sky that rests over 'the Wagait', one of the most contested areas in Australia. Once this was Indigenous people's land, in all the complexity of that land tenure system. Since late in the nineteenth century, invasion by European and Chinese settlers, and by feral plants and animals, has resulted in a multiplicity of land-use objectives. These include pastoralism, mining, tourism, conservation and reclamation, along with Indigenous subsistence and land care. With conquest, parts of the area were reserved for Aboriginal people; and when the Australian nation decided to move beyond its colonial regime by granting unconditional citizenship and land rights to Aboriginal people, the former reserve became the site of an intensely bitter dispute amongst Aboriginal people.

As the Mak Mak state, they, the white-breasted sea-eagle clan, have lived here since time immemorial. This is their country — their life, law and land. They were a party to the land rights dispute, and are now secure in their tenure of a portion of their traditional homelands.

We invite you to travel with us, and share in some of the love and care that keeps this country alive.

The evening sky above the Wagait.

The floodplains.

The Florence River coming down off the range.

The Tabletop Range is hill country, where the rivers start up. Range country holds the water in swamps where the springs bubble up and the rivers flow all year round. The Florence River flows into the Finniss, and the Finniss flows to the sea. These are northern tropical rivers, huge in the wet season and smaller in the Dry, roaring down off the hills and meandering across the plains.

Out on those floodplains the water slows down. The tides reach in to the land, and the rivers struggle to find the sea. Huge paperbark swamps and billabongs hold the water, and the rivers bend and twist as they work their way westward.

Here and there are small rainforests — the 'wet' and 'dry' jungles whose existence depends upon Aboriginal care of country.

Florence Falls (left).

The 'eye' of the spring.

Inside a wet jungle you can see a place within the spring where the water actually comes up out of the ground. Mak Mak people call that the 'eye' — the 'eye' of the spring.

There are 'eyes' all over this country; this is a place where living things take notice of each other. People travel across the land, and they watch, observe, remember, think about and tell stories. Other living things watch too; they all watch, observe, think and tell stories. This place is sentient.

Jungles and billabongs: A billabong (pictured left) is a waterhole in the anabranch of a river, and is replenished by rainwater and floods. North Australian jungles are remnant patches of rainforest. These small ecosystems have survived since ancient times, and contain the main species of terrestrial vegetation found in Australia and South-East Asia. Mak Mak people classify the jungles as either wet or dry, depending on whether there is permanent water in the jungle.[2]

To gain a sense of how things 'tie in together', let's go back to the high country. In the time of creation, according to Aboriginal people, the great creator beings, called 'Dreamings', were travelling and making the world. Old Man Goose was up in the high country. When the rains stopped and the floodplains began to dry out, Old Man Goose started calling out for everybody to come for a ceremony. He made the river as he came walking and calling across the country. Old Man Goose is one of the many creator beings who brought place and people, species, actions and order into being.

Kathy: It's like the spider: A lot of things tie in together, so when you ask one thing, you get a whole big history.

Kathy Deveraux.

Old Man Karramala, as Old Man Goose is called in the language of the Mak Mak people, started at the top of the range, and came striding down calling to other Dreamings in the region. He thus bestrode the two main portions of the clan's country: the highlands and the floodplains. For millennia, life in this region has consisted of seasonal movement to the high country during the wet season and back out onto the floodplains in the dry season. This is how life is lived: when the plains are underwater, the people are on the ridges and hills. As the plains dry out, people and other living things move out onto them.

Old Man Goose was walking to a place called Djulurrk (which is a billabong near the Finniss River). He came striding along, playing the didjeridu and calling all the creatures to come together for ceremony (see Map of Mak Mak Dreamings, p. xiii). The sound of the didjeridu is unmistakable. If you have heard the songs and been in the ceremonies, the distinctive music makes your body want to jump up and dance.[3]

The didjeridu is called *kenbi* in Mak Mak (Marranunggu) and related languages, and at Djulurrk there are dense stands of bamboo, also called *kenbi*. Formerly, the didjeridu was made of bamboo. The term *kenbi* thus refers both to the plant and to the instrument, although the didjeridu is most often made now from the hollow branches of a eucalyptus tree, and only rarely from bamboo.

Didjeridu made by Nancy Daiyi as a gift for Linda Ford. Nancy used the hollow log of a gum tree (Eucalyptus phoenicia).

Didjeridu: A musical instrument made from a hollowed piece of bamboo, or a hollowed log. Resin or beeswax is applied around the mouthpiece, and the instrument is played by breathing a continuous stream of air through the instrument while vibrating the lips. Once restricted to an area from the Gulf of Carpentaria across the north into Western Australia, the didjeridu has become an international instrument communicating a new tribalism. Within Australia, both the instrument and the music are prominent icons signalling Aboriginality.[4]

Kathy: *Djulburr is the goose. Old Man Karramala we call him.*

Kathy: *That's where the Florence Falls come from ~ Old Man Karramala.*

Djulburr blowing his kenbi.

Florence Falls — Djulburr, Old Man Karramala (Goose) blows his kenbi *and makes Florence Falls.*

Kathy: Florence Falls. Goose Dreaming. Where Djulburr been blow *kenbi*, make a waterfall. That is where the goose story starts, there now.

And all down Florence Creek, *Paekurrimala* we call it: he was walking there. Where the goose been go, [he] went on his merry way down to the junction, making this creek.

That place is Djulurrk. That's bamboo there. We call the bamboo *kenbi*. Old man Karramala must have planted them. *Kenbi* goes with Goose Dreaming. Proper goose, he's a *Kenbi* man. He's got a honker!

So, Old Man Karramala blew his didjeridu (*kenbi*), making the rivers as he walked to Djulurrk, which is a major resource site for bamboo (*kenbi*).

Djulburr walking along makes Paekurrimala (Florence Creek).

Australian bamboo: (*Bambusa arnhemica*) is regarded by botanists as endemic to a small area in the north-west corner of the Northern Territory. It grows along banks and fringes of lowland freshwater streams and in associated jungle. As it grows only along a restricted number of river systems, and is highly prized by Aboriginal people, it was and is today a major trade item.[5]

Djulurrk, where Djulburr planted bamboo.

This sacred geography is all here today. Old Man Goose made the Florence River, and it joins the Finniss River which was made by the Rainbow Serpent as it moved across the country. Djulurrk is a sacred site as well as a resource site. All across the Wagait, and all across Australia, geography has its origins in the sacred work of creation.

HOMELANDS

Kathy: I ask Mum, 'When you travel around other places for ceremonies, down to the Daly River to the outstations ... how do you compare their country with yours?' Her reply: 'I feel like a foreigner because **my heart doesn't belong to their country**'.[6]

When Europeans arrived in Australia, and as they explored the continent, they thought they were in a wilderness. In fact, the continent was a series of homes, each one cared for by the Aboriginal people who possessed the rights and duties of care because they belonged there.

An understanding of 'country', for those of us who were not born and raised to it, starts with the idea that country is a nourishing terrain.[7] Country is a place that gives and receives life. Not just imagined or represented, it is both lived in and lived with.

In Aboriginal English, the word 'country' is both a common noun and a proper noun. People talk about country in the same way that they would talk about a person: they speak to country, sing to country, visit country, worry about country, grieve for country and long for country. People say that country knows, hears, smells, takes notice, takes care, is sorry or happy. Country is a living entity with a yesterday, today and tomorrow, with consciousness, action, and a will toward life. Because of this richness of meaning, country is home and peace; nourishment for body, mind and spirit; and heart's ease.

Everywhere one goes in Aboriginal Australia, people describe their own homeland as 'good country'. From the bleakest sand hills to mosquito-infested swamps, each homeland is 'good country' for the people who belong there.

April Bright describes what 'traditional ownership' meant to her mother. She wanted to explain her mother's life, and in so doing, she was also explaining her own life:

April: Traditional ownership to country for my Mum was everything ~ everything. It was the songs, the ceremony, the land, themselves, their family ~ everything that life was all about. This place here was her heart. That's what she lived for, and that's what she died for.[8]

April: This place was her heart.

Didjini billabong.

Action — Connection

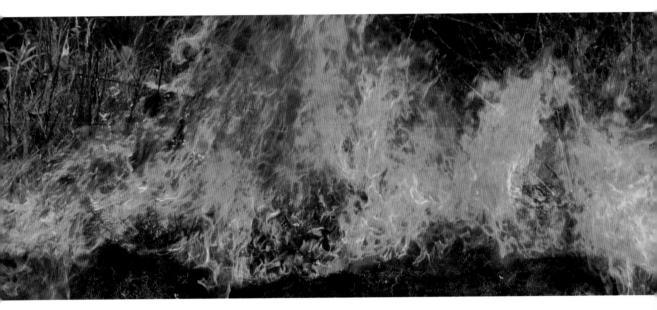

'...This is the time we burn our country. It is
part of our responsibility in looking after country
... The country tells you when and where to burn.

April Bright

INTERCONNECTION

In this place — this ecological web called 'country' — living things interact. Their lives are interconnected because they are here together in this place. In the same way, their stories interconnect, past connects with present, and creation is part of the contemporary life of the place and its people.

Here, everything came into being by Dreaming, and indigenous living things exist because of, and through, relationships established by Dreaming. The places where Dreamings travelled, where they stopped and where they lived the events of their lives and deaths are tracks and sites. The creation stories vividly recount the actions and events that brought a particular place, ceremony, group of people or kind of action into being.

One part of the Djulurrk story tells how the Rainbow Snake (PuleyPuley) stole fire. The Dreamings were doing ceremony at Djulurrk, and the Rainbow Snake took the fire in his mouth and went racing away to find the sea so that he could drown the fire. He went this way and that, twisting across the land trying to reach the sea, but before he could drown the fire forever, another Dreaming — the Chickenhawk, *a-titit* (*Accipiter fasciatus*) — came chasing after him. He grabbed the firestick from PuleyPuley and flew away with it. *a-titit* saved fire for the world; without his actions, there would be no fire. As he flew with the firestick he had taken from the Rainbow Snake, he dropped sparks across the land. As *a-titit* scattered fire, he inaugurated the use of fire in the land.

Kathy: And 'burn grass time', you look: *a-titit*. Chickenhawk. You blame him for making fire, because he dropped that fire. He took it off the Rainbow Snake, PuleyPuley, and made fire everywhere.

They been come for ceremony. And, Dancing Man, *a-titit*, Chickenhawk. Him been dancing bird. PuleyPuley got wild, that's the Rainbow Snake, and took it away that fire. And *a-titit* come and got it off him.

Linda: Next thing, *a-karrk* (brown falcon) stole it off him and went and burnt Marenja Hill (see pp. 136–137).

A-karrk *(brown falcon)* Falco berigora.

CULTURAL FIRES

You first sense the coming of the dry season in the monsoonal tropics of Australia when a breath of air touches your skin with a slightly fresh and cool texture. Almost at the same time, you smell a dryness that whispers of smoke, ash and eucalyptus oils. Your heart lifts, and you know that the Indigenous peoples have started burning the country.

'Cultural fires' is the term used to discriminate between wild fires and fires deliberately started and managed. It has taken white settlers, scientists and others a very long time to appreciate the fact that Indigenous peoples in Australia (and elsewhere) consciously manage their country through the expert use of fire.[9]

Recent studies of Aboriginal people's pro-active care of Australian fauna, flora and ecosystems have begun to demonstrate how widespread, knowledgeable and influential these land and resource management practices have always been. It is becoming increasingly evident to scientists that both the distribution and the diversity of Australian biota across the continent are artefacts of Aboriginal people's intentional fires.[10]

Many Australian plants require fire either to flower, or for their seeds to germinate. Likewise, many animals also depend on, or respond well to, the effects of fire. Certainly, catastrophic firestorms do not promote the life of ecosystems. Aboriginal burning practices are based on patch-burning, however, selectively using low and high intensity fires as appropriate, so that people sustain a mosaic of habitats over a number of years. Proper burning regimes require detailed knowledge of the terrain and of a range of local factors such as prevailing winds, plant communities and the fire history of particular places. Aboriginal cultural fire regimes are thus implemented by the people who have the responsibility for, and the knowledge of, the country.

Margy Daiyi starting fires in dry grass. Margy is Kathy Deveraux's sister.

Margy: A hot fire. And you can see how its little wings are all breaking away from the main fire.

In most parts of Australia, when Aboriginal people speak English, they describe their burning practices as 'cleaning up the country'.[11] There is a well-defined aesthetic: country which has been burned is country which looks cared for and clean. It is good country because, if you know how to see, you can see that people are taking care of it. As April Bright explains, ' ... if we don't burn our country every year, we are not looking after our country'.[12]

~

Margy: That's a hot fire. You can tell by the height of the flames, and you can see how its little wings are all breaking away from the main fire. There's hardly any smoke. And you can tell there's a wind behind it. It's standing up, and it's leaning.

Kathy: It's running. You can tell it's running. It's running toward the right from that little thing on the left. You can see it's leaning toward the right, that flame lying down and running.

April Bright. In the kinship system, April is Kathy and Margy's sister.

Margy: See, [right] it's going into the paperbark. You can see a wind behind there. See how the flames are sort of spindly up top? The fire roared through there. Those little puffs of smoke will be all that mulch. All the dead sticks and wallaby turd, just ashes, just ashes burning.

Kathy: And, see the flames leaping up top there, see?

Margy: The fire's going past that tree now. There's a lot of fuel in there. The wind is fairly getting behind this fire too, getting behind the flame. It's run up that tree, that flame. Straight up the paperbark.

April: 'Burn grass': this is what we call the procedure of burning off our country. We call it, simply, 'burn grass' or 'burn grass time'. This is the time we burn our country. It is part of our responsibility in looking after our country. If you don't look after country, country won't look after you.

'Burn grass' is as ancient as time itself. Very briefly, the Chickenhawk ~ *a-titit* ~ took a firestick from a fire that was lit for a big ceremony and flew across Kurrindju, and as he flew across the country he burnt it.

'Burn grass' takes place after the wet season when the grass starts drying off. This takes place every year. The country tells you when and where to burn. To carry out this task you must know your country. You wouldn't, you just would not attempt to burn someone else's country. One of the reasons for burning is saving country. If we don't burn our country every year, we are not looking after our country. Right across our country we have very dense grasses, even in the ranges and timbered areas. If our country wasn't burnt, then spear grass, anything up to ten feet high, other dense grasses, leaves and fallen branches would form a thick underlying mat of mulch, even in as little as three to five years. If a fire was lit either purposely or through natural causes, especially through the height of the dry season, it would do untold damage to the flora and fauna. The ecosystem would suffer. The country would be burnt to a crisp.[13]

Fire in the paperbark.

Kathy: The fire's been and gone [right], only the ashes and smoke and little bit of dead wood burning. See it's still green? That's a clean burn. It's taken out most of the scrub, the vines, the long grass, any old stumps or sticks, all gone. All cleaned up. You can travel through it faster and quicker, and you can see more and longer. Not just us, but animals too.

See, the fire didn't burn right up the tree. The foliage is still green. The fire didn't strip the foliage, it just burnt this little bit of bark. It won't kill the tree. Might be this year or next year, you'll see all the little suckers coming up.

There you can see why we call it a clean burn. See all this dry grass in the front, see all the vines and that. You can see where it's burnt, it's all cleaned out. That's what we mean. Cleaned. Get rid of all the junk in the front. And we can access the paperbark without worrying about tripping over grass and falling on snakes.

The term 'cultural fire' connotes human agency, but the fires of North Australia are more complex than that, as the story of the Chickenhawk tells us. Smoke is part of a communicative web in which many living things are involved and pay attention. The firebirds sense the smoke and come circling around, preparing to dive in as soon as there is an opportunity. Some of them are fire-makers themselves. They swoop down, grab a firestick, carry it away, and drop it ahead of the fire, thus encouraging it to keep moving:

Kathy: The *a-karrk* is like a falcon. It's a bandit. It likes to hang around fires, you know. Like when there's a bushfire, well, we say that bandit, he starts all the fires, because that's where they get their feed from, when that fire makes all that smoke and they find all the tucker and that for themself.[14]

Margy: Where there's fire, there's hawks.

Firebirds: In North Australia several species of raptors use the zone of a fire as a prime hunting ground. Brown and black falcons attend and wait for the small animals that try to escape. Whistling kites (*Haliastur sphenurus*) and black kites circle around and dive down for insects and fleeing animals. Other birds attend: kestrel, buzzards, harriers and crows. Yet another suite of birds moves in after the fire, feeding on seeds that are more readily found then.[15]

Whistling kite.

Kathy: That's the whistling kite flying in the smoke. In the Dreamtime story, when there's a fire, you see big mob of those. And when he sings out, we whistle too. We encourage him.

Nancy: And then the flames come more high. He's the fire man.

Kathy: We get excited for the fire. That's the fire whistle we make. And he whistles, he's excited over the fire. This is the whistling kite: *a-pelele*.

~

Margy: That's nice. Just how the flames are dancing around that place (right). You can still see the flame inside there, look.

And with fire like that you stand and you whistle to make the fire more high. And it goes higher and higher and harder and faster.

Kathy: And you jump up and down and sing out 'hooray'.

Margy: With fire like that you stand and whistle to make the fire more high (right).

'...a clean burn'

Kathy

Kathy: That's what we call a clean burn. Cycad leaves burnt. And all leaves fall off, and not long after this now you get the green shoots coming off the tops. They get new foliage. When it starts fogging up.

Margy: It's recent. See the ashes.

Kathy: It's clean. All the scrub's gone. You can see the country, you can see where you're going.

Margy: Not a blade of grass.

Linda: It's been burnt back to the stubble.

Kathy: That's what we mean by 'clean burn'.

The same cycads (right) two weeks later.

White apple in flower:
Mimumbudi (Syzygium
eucalyptoides).

Many Australian plants are fire-adapted, and thus actually depend on fire for the completion of their life cycle. Other plants are fire-sensitive, and would suffer greatly if caught in a huge firestorm. The jungles, for example, are relic rainforests whose survival has depended upon Aboriginal burning.[16] Mak Mak people's burning strategies respond to the needs of both groups. Mak Mak burning protects the plants or plant communities that would be harmed by harsh fires, and provides fire for those plants and plant communities that require it.

Some 'burns' are directed toward management of harvest. White apples, for example, produce fruit within a time frame linked to when they were burnt. Thus, many small burns will spread out the harvest of white apples, allowing people to go on harvesting them over a long period of time.

The zamia palm, also known as the 'cycad' (*Cycus armstrongii*, *Cycus calciola*), is a North Australian plant that shows just how fire-adapted some living things can become. It is an ancient species, and its poisonous seeds must be subjected to long and complicated processing to render them edible. Cycads can be fired to produce a large harvest simultaneously, and the food was a staple for provisioning large groups that gathered for ceremony. The planning involved was extensive, and included organising the ceremony; 'firing' the cycads; sending messengers with invitations; and harvesting large amounts of cycad nuts, processing them and cooking them for the guests.

Linda: Cycad nuts. Cycads, zamia tree, female and male. That's a female.

Kathy: *Mirrwana* is the tree, and *pelangu* is the big nut that comes off when they're green. You soak them. You bust it open and get the smaller nut on the inside. That's the tucker [food]. You roll them up in paperbark and you put the bundle in water for one or two weeks. Billabong water. It attracts the blowflies because it smells like shit! Anyway, take out the tucker, and grind the nut to make a flour. Add water, get a big leaf, spread it out like a pancake, and put it on the ashes. Cover it over and cook it a little bit. Take it out when it's cooked. It's black as black. It comes out like a bread. And it still smells like shit! It tastes all right. Sweet. It tastes good.

Nancy: Emus eat it too. Sometimes we used to pick those nuts up out of the emu shit. We get that nut again, we bust it up, we open it up and we eat it, that *miyi* [food from a plant].

Kathy: They were sharing with emus. They scrounge it out of the emu shit and cook it up for themselves. Because it hasn't been digested. It's still inside the kernels. Emu eats only the outer flesh, but we eat the inside one tucker. My grandfather, Old Wigma [see Genealogical Sketch, p. xii], he cooked it on a leaf and gave it to me ...

We all laughed when Kathy told this story so vividly. Of course, funny stories can also refer to important and serious connections.

Kathy went on to remark, 'Nancy is emu. Did you know that?'

Emu (*Dromaius novae-hollandiae*).

Nancy Daiyi. The emu is Nancy's mirr.

COMING INTO BEING

Country brings its people into being. The Mak Mak term for this is *mirr*. It denotes a relationship of consubstantiality (or shared substance) between the person and place, and the species from which their being comes forth.

Knowledge of this intimate connection arrives in the form of an unusual event. A person knows their *mirr* (species and place) because something occurred that stood out from the ordinary. This event 'told' the mother, the maternal grandmother or another close woman about an unborn child. Through *mirr*, each person is connected in an unpredictable and unique way to their world:

Margy: My youngest son Calvin, his Aboriginal name is Muluk. That [place] is down on the beach. Because I saw a big croc there, and later on a few days after that, my husband Colin was commercial fishing with Dad and he caught a 16–17 foot salt water crocodile in the net. Mum told him that I was pregnant. So the crocodile is Calvin's *mirr*.[17]

Kathy: Salt water crocodile there [right]. A proper saltie. We've got the two kinds of crocodiles, the two man-eating crocodiles, and one of them is called *a-kenbi* because of those yellow patches [that look like bamboo]. This one here is the golden one: fresh water/salt water man-eating stumpy-nosed 'gator.

Rankin Deveraux (Kathy's son) has a similar story that connects him with a large and dangerous hill, as well as with a large and dangerous predator.

Calvin Deveraux.

'My youngest son Calvin "Muluk" ... crocodile is Calvin's mirr.'

Margy

Rankin Deveraux. In the kinship system, Rankin is Calvin's brother.

Rankin: My name is Ngalgal and that's my Dreaming, that hill. How I got my name was my uncle and Dad were up there waiting for the tide to go out and a big black salt water croc popped up, and when they got back to the camp they told Nana [Nancy] and Nana asked Mum [Kathy] if she was pregnant and Mum said yes, she was. So that's how I got my name ~ Ngalgal ~ from that hill over there.[18]

Crocodiles: Scientists identify two species of crocodile in Australia. *Crocodylus johnstoni* is the smaller 'fresh water' or 'fish' croc and is endemic. *Crocodylus porosus* is the larger 'salt water' croc, and is found from India across South-East Asia, Papua New Guinea and Australia. *C. porosus* is a killer. Mak Mak people make a further distinction within this species, as they identify two types of salt water crocodile. As the billabongs dry out, crocodiles must either migrate or bury themselves in the mud and wait for rain.[19]

Saltwater crocodile.

Linda Ford — Linda's mirr is kugun *(native honey). Linda is Nancy's daughter, and Kathy and Margaret's sister. (Photo by D. Rose)*

(left) Kugan *in the paperbark trees.*

Linda: I can relate my experience through my *mirr*, which is *kugun*. *Kugun* is the native sugarbag that is full of wild honey, produced by a native honey bee that looks similar to a small house fly. *Wuwe ngany ka mirr* [my conception place is] Wuntyityi, Wadanang, near the junction of Paekurrimala on the Finniss River. How do I know this? My mother told me! Who told her? The clan's midwife! She is incredibly knowledgeable about all matters in relation to the land, other natural elements of science and the spiritual signs. Mum's midwife was *Attyang* Nginyiwal. She was my *Unga's* [great uncle's] wife from my mother's *marrithiel* [language/tribe] side, and she foresaw the changes in the pregnancies of her daughters.[20]

I'm native honey.

There's sugarbag in those paperbark trees. All through that country there. And the place called Kugun is over on the other side. Kugun, we call it. That means sugarbag. That's me. *Kugun* is my *mirr*. I'm wild honey.'

Country thus impels itself into women in order to bring new human life into the world. The relationship is interactive. Women who are in the country — burning, fishing, hunting, getting other foods, visiting places and observing what is going on — are available to the agency of country. People's daily interactions with country provide the context in which the bringing forth of new life occurs.

'Country Tells You'

'When I travel around my country I won't starve. I know I'll find good tucker because I have the right sweat for my country. It'll look after us, because we are one and the same. You only need to call out. Talk to the land, it gives us life.'

Nancy Daiyi

COMMUNICATING WITH COUNTRY

Kathy: Travelling through the bush, we catch a whiff of a refreshingly sweet smell. *Nyaa*, we say as we deeply inhale the tantalising perfumes released by Mother Nature. This is our way of describing the delicious scents mingling in the air. The smell of the bush is therapeutic, healing and soothing mind, body and soul. *Wana thawarr mitiyin kemina* [just like medicine]. You don't stay away for very long, do you?

Nancy: No. I can never stay too long. Otherwise I will get properly homesick. I mean really sick. I miss the smell and the sound of the swamp and all the activities and characteristics of the animals. I can picture them. My senses taste the sweet smell of the *memeken* [floating grass] on the billabongs when it gets burnt and starts shooting again. The fat from our turtle, geese and barramundi is not the same anywhere else in the world.[21]

Country produces a communicative web. It talks about itself all the time, and its language is sensual. Taste, touch, sound and sight reverberate to the messages that country gives out. Communication arises among the living things, including human beings, who are part of this system. People give out sensual messages too.

Through *mirr*, each Mak Mak person is consubstantial with a species and place. As the person lives, they move through their country: from place to place, from event to event. Country knows people by their history and their presence; and by their sweat, which is a manifestation of their unique essence. People work, their sweat goes into the country, and the country knows them. People talk, cry, call out, laugh, and the country comes to know them. Thus, a lifetime of action inscribes the person into the country as part of its being, its story and its communicative web.

Kathy: Nancy cries out one long and loud 'Yuu'. We pause for a moment, look toward her as she acknowledges the home of our ancestors for reassurance, then carry on with whatever we're doing. When the tide turns and the breeze comes, she talks to the wind; *Yigaiiii*, she says, meaning 'Ahh what a relief, this feels so good'. From nowhere, a whirly-whirly kicks up its heels and starts a dust storm beside her. She growls at it and beckons it to go away. *Tyuk*. She curses it with fine spit and directs it with a show of jerky arm movements and a string of real curses, so it can disperse.[22]

Mak Mak people know their country, and their country knows them. Not only are they brought into being by the country, but their daily and yearly interactions with country are communicative events. In calling to the country, lighting fires, cooking food, laughing and singing, they communicate their presence to country. Mak Mak people are known individually by their sweat, and when strangers come, Mak Mak people introduce them to the country through a brief ritual that mingles the sweat of the newcomer with the sweat of a Mak Mak person. When the stranger is washed in water, their sweat goes into the river systems and is dispersed on the air, so that country will know them.

Nancy: When I travel around my country I won't starve. I know I'll find good tucker because I have the right sweat for my country. It'll look after us, because we are one and the same. You only need to call out. Talk to the land, it gives us life.[23]

If it takes people being in country for country to impel itself into people, it also takes knowledge for people to be in country. Westerners may think of such connections as mystical or spiritual, and perhaps they are; but it seems enormously significant that they come into being in the most mundane actions of daily life. As Beth Povinelli writes of the neighbouring Belyuen people: ' ... all hunting trips interact with the sentient landscape, and the sentient landscape most commonly encounters humans engaged in economic, not ritual, activity.'[24]

For Mak Mak people, interactions with country that take place in daily life are called forth by country. April explained this when she said, ' ... country tells you where and when to burn.' Many of the Mak Mak people's actions are organised around the messages of country that, for knowledgeable people, are calls to action.

Kathy: You got to *bogey* [bathe]. Bogey your sweat. So you can't get sick or you can't get hurt. When a stranger come, we *djukpi*. Put 'em water. *Djukpi* means wet their head, for walking through that country.

'That's mum introducing Debbie to Country'

Linda

Nancy Daiyi introduced Debbie Rose to the country in 1993. Linda Ford assisted, with Calvin Deveraux watching. (Photo by M. Daiyi)

TIME

When you travel, you move through time as well as through country. Different cultures understand time differently. Contemporary western concepts of time rest on ancient Greek ideas of the cyclical 'time' of nature, and the linear 'time' of mortal life.[25] Some authors have suggested that Greek thought spatialises time, expressing concepts of time in geometric terms (circles and lines).[26] In Greek thought, the most valued human actions were held to run counter to nature, and enduring monuments were erected that resisted the cycles of nature. According to Arendt: ' ... The mortality of man lies in the fact that individual life ... rises out of biological life ... This is mortality: to move along a rectilinear line in a universe where everything, if it moves at all, moves in a cyclical order'.[27]

Modern western culture has re-thought many of the qualities of mortality and nature, without discarding the geometric structures and the concept of action that sets 'man' in opposition to nature. In modernity, human life seeks to intervene to control nature; we not only construct monuments that will endure against the entropy of the natural world, but we also control life processes in defiance of entropy. Modern thought paradigmatically refers to two types of 'time': linear and cyclical (time's arrow and time's circle).

Characteristically, western modernism asserts that cyclical time typifies
non-western peoples.

In contrast, Mak Mak people's thinking about time is attuned to ecological
time, and thus is too complex to be reduced to circles and lines.[28] The
communicative system of country embraces rhythms and beats, as well as
cycles and returns. Here, human life is oriented toward working *with* these
rhythms, not against them. Again, knowledge is the key. The rhythms of
simultaneous events are critical codes for knowing what is currently happening,
and how one is to act. Some of this knowledge is dispersed widely, and some
is highly localised. Many of the signs of concurrence vary from place to place,
so that one really only knows what is happening in the places where one has
the knowledge of the concurrences that exist and of their meanings. When
Nancy spoke of feeling like a foreigner in neighbouring country, she said, ' ...
I feel very vulnerable for I have not the same intimate knowledge they have for
their land, just as they do not have for mine.'

Events that occur to the same rhythm also require intervals. There are
times when things do not happen, and it is the 'not-happening' that makes
it possible for the 'happening' to have meaning. For example, dragonflies
announce the beginning of the Dry by their appearance *en masse*; this
appearance is only noticeable because for a long time they have not been
around in any great numbers at all. Similarly, the arrival of the fireflies tells
you that goose eggs and salt water crocodile eggs are ready to harvest; and
when the march flies arrive, this tells you that the wet season is coming and
the barramundi are biting.

Such signs are not inherently linked to an external frame of reference,
although Mak Mak people also organise their actions with regard to school
schedules, public holidays and a forty-hour work week. One of the merits of a
wholly internal system is its consistency. Unlike arbitrary calendars,
concurrent ecological events work to their own stimulus and response,
interacting with the world around them. The dragonflies may stand on grass
that has been drenched by rain, but their presence is telling you that the dry
season is starting.

Beat and interval, presence and absence, departure and return, actions and
connections ... Mak Mak time concepts do not suggest that human life goes
against the grain of nature. Rather, these time concepts link the body — with
its heartbeat and other rhythms — with country. To find the beat, pay attention
to the world. Time here is about periodicity, attention, action and connection.

[handwritten margin note: based on sun & moon cycles, too? maybe just more flexible to Change comp. to "universal" Calendars]

'Burn grass time, when the seeds are gone — they already tried to burn here, but they burnt too early.'

Margy

Margy: It's nearly 'burn grass'. The grass is bent over. All the seeds are gone. The seed is finished.

And it goes brown and dry. In the wet season it's tall and green and full of life.

See here, they already tried to burn there, but they burnt too early. The grass didn't get burnt properly. They'll have to burn again later on, when it's properly dry. It was too green when they burnt it. It still had a lot of moisture, a lot of green. And when it gets really dry, you can burn that again, and it'll make it really clean. You'll get a clean burn later.

The grass starts to dry out, even while the rain continues (left).

'New shoots coming up after burn grass time.'

Margy and April

Margy: Those little green clumps come up really sweet and clean. And it feeds the wallabies.

April: 'Burn grass time' gives us good hunting. It brings animals such as wallabies, kangaroos and turkeys onto the new fresh feed of green grasses and plants. But it does not only provide for us but also for animals, birds, reptiles and insects. After the 'burn' you will see hundreds of white cockatoos digging for grass roots. It's quite funny because they are no longer snow white but have blackened heads, and undercarriages black from the soot. The birds fly to the smoke to snatch up insects. Wallabies, kangaroos, bandicoots, birds, rats, mice, reptiles and insects all access these areas for food. If it wasn't burnt they would not be able to penetrate the dense and long spear grass and other grasses for these sources of food.

Kathy: Thudungu/thudungawa [dragonfly] [left]. That's beautiful. That's the start of the Dry. The dragonfly tells you.

We follow the receding waters over our country. As the water dries up on top of the soil and the grass is dry enough to ignite, we burn. These areas are usually the low lying areas between hills and ridges. We call them 'flats'. The fires bring the moisture to the surface from under the soil, drying up the land for access and to feed the grass and plants into new growth.

Winds are very important to fire burning. There are different winds for different burns.

Big winds: Big winds will spread the fires rapidly, burning dry grasses, leaves and some dead wood. The fire being pushed by these winds does not allow for severe damage to take place on the grasses, plants and trees. The effect would be like passing your hands through the flame of a candle. You'll feel the heat but your hands will not blister.

Slow winds: This is very little wind. Just enough to keep the fires burning. We call this 'slow burn' or 'colder burn'. These burns take place around areas you want to protect, like areas of significance or also areas like the rainforest. The floors of these rainforests are dense with rotting vegetation and if burnt with hot fires or at the wrong time they will burn and smoulder for weeks, causing extensive damage to the undergrowth and the life forms in it.

The slow burns usually take place [in the] very late afternoon knowing that as night approaches the wind will cease and the fires die out. These can be lit during the day if no winds are around at all. The most important thing with this burn is [that] you are able to control the fire. It is easily put out with leafy branches when you don't want it to burn.

Hot burns are later. These are lit when the ridge country is dry. The hot fires sweep hard and fast over these areas. The trees and plants in these areas are protected by their bark and they're usually hard timbered. The nut fruits are also very hard, where you need a stone to crack them open. The hot fires assist them to burst, allowing the seeds to regenerate. A lot of the trees produce suckers, regrowth of the roots. We refer to them as suckers.

A good portion of our country is floodplains and paperbark swamps. These areas are the last to dry up after the Wet. These areas are burnt like the 'flat areas'. There's still a lot of water under the soil.

Some areas that look like land are really masses of floating grass. These areas are burnt hotly before it becomes too dry. The burning takes place before the turtles hibernate. As the billabongs and channels drop their water levels, the turtles bury themselves in the mud. This takes place only in certain areas. The grasses on these plains are very dense.[29]

Wallabies.

Goanna.

Margy: And it feeds the wallabies.

Kathy: They all come back for a feed when it gets green. Goannas, goannas walk around in fresh green. Everything comes to life after that first burn.

Burn grass time is also sugarbag time:

Margy: When you burn the grass, the silky oak flowers, and that's when you go out and get sugarbag.

Termites: In the tropical ecosystem termites have a large role in nutrient recycling. Those termites which build their nests as mounds ('antbeds' in Aboriginal English) enrich the soil in their immediate area, and deplete resources in the areas in which they salvage. In a survey of an area of Kakadu National Park, scientists found 50 species, of which 15 were mound builders.[31]

Kathy: *Wunthawu* [antbed]. This is a big antbed [termite mound]. You get sugarbag in them antbeds because they're mostly hollow inside. You can get it anywhere from around the bottom, to the middle, to the top. You just walk round and round it, and you'll see that little 'eye', and the bees buzzing around. And you got your honey.

Margy: Yes, sunlight coming through, drying out all that wet grass.

Sugarbag: Throughout Australia, Aboriginal people use the term 'sugarbag' to refer to native honey. Native bees of Australia belong to the Trigona species. They are a social species; each nest contains the queen, the workers and the drones. The bees are small, black or brown, and cannot sting.[30]

Margy: Sugarbag in the zamia palm [cycad]. I took honey out of that, and put the wood back, and it kept on going. It's made new honey because a little bit got left behind so the bees make new honey.

Kathy: After it burns, all the new shoots come up straight away. Might be one week, and it's all green again. From that thelbek [fogs], from the big fogs in the dry season that make the green come back. And sometimes the ground is still wet, anyway.

Nancy: Bushfire makes the colour like that.

Kurrajong
[Brachychiton].

Nancy: That's from bush fire, he get colour like that. Smoke make it go that colour. 'Im been makembat colour like that.

Kathy: Palm fronds there. You can tell it's up on the range because of the palm fronds. It's up pretty high, and looking down.

~

Kathy: *Kurrajong* [*Brachychiton*] [left]. We eat that. It's got little nuts inside: *nanarra*. It's just like a peanut, all that nut inside. And it's got really fine prickles, hair, like a caterpillar, so you have to cook it in the fire. See that pod, they sit in there like little peas. And it's the pods, the casings, that are hairy. But the nuts are really nice. It's just like peanut, all that nut inside.

Margy: This lily with a red-pink flower is *miperiya* [*Nymphaea violacea*] [right]. You can eat it: stem, roots and seeds. It tastes oily, that seed. Looks like shotgun pellets, they're a steel grey colour. The whole thing tastes oily, like grapeseed oil.

Kathy: If you inhale it, it's got eucalyptus smells. The stalk is like celery. And you can feel for the root (the corm) with your feet. Hold the stem, and feel it, and pull it out. It's proper tucker.

Miperiya [*lily*, Nymphaea violacea].

Margy: Nengmerra *[young geese]. Three young geese. They've just finished hatching. They start mating November/December, got chickens by March/April.*

Margy: Calvin the hunter. He's my son. Calvin's getting a feed of djulburr [goose].

Stiff, cracked black soil.

Thunderclouds heralding wurrum, *the big Wet.*

Kathy: Soon it will be *wurrum* [the big wet season]. The stiff, cracked, black soil plains wait in anticipation for the early rains. The smell of rain on a dry earth has an awesome affect on people, flora and fauna. It's an earthy smell that is almost edible, it can be tasted on the wind. It's a sign of continuity, a happy time. A time to prepare for the Wet, taking refuge along the escarpment.[32]

~

Kathy: It's early December and the air is thick with the fragrant smell of ripened little sweet green plums and shiny black plums. Passing by, you make a mental note of the area and revisit later on, where they can be found in abundance ... [there are] pretty new colours, growth and appealing smells.[33]

Lightning over the floodplains.

Pandanus in the rain.

'Is it a girl tree or a male
tree? You can tell
by the spiral?'

Linda

'It's got big nuts!'

Kathy

Kathy: During the wet season, when all the floodplains are underwater, most of the food sources are sought on the ridges and the hill country, and when the country dries out around about Easter time, and water starts slowing down and starts drying up a little bit, we move back onto the plains and start fishing and getting turtles and goose eggs.[34]

Paperbark swamp in flood.

Dry season paperback swamp.

'Underneath the
water is grass,
onion grass.'

Kathy

Kathy: The water is that clear, you're seeing all the grass knocked over with the current. Underneath the water is grass, onion grass.

~

Linda: That's the river covered up with floating grass [right]. *Memeken*. It's covered with floating grass.

Margy: We used to drive the cattle across, but you have to know where to go, or you'll fall through. If you fall in, it'll close up over you and you'll be croc bait. There's layers of grass and mud, and water underneath.

Memeken *(floating grass)*.

Dragonfly — signalling the start of the Dry.

Kathy: Dragonfly ~ that tells you big mob fish, barramundi, everything. Fishing time. Start of the Dry. Start of the Dry, when they come out, dragonfly. You start to get itchy feet yourself. Itchy to go fishing.

ACTION

Kathy: An exceptionally good hunter–gatherer is known to have *milityin* powers. They are regarded highly for their hunting prowess in providing food for the camp. A *milityin* [a person who is a great hunter] rarely comes back empty-handed. At home in their element, they have the natural ability to find food. When hunting wild game, the *milityin* may not only have to consider where a barramundi or long-neck turtle may be resting in the middle of a hot day, but must take extra precautions for the big crocodile who regularly cruises up and down his territory. A *milityin* has to out-think and out-smart them all.[35]

The food that people get when they go hunting is consumed, and the remains are handled with respect. When Nancy goes fishing, she cooks the fish on the coals, and then she burns the bones. The reason?

Nancy: Because it come from that country, so we leave 'im there, burn 'im up.[36]

Nancy Daiyi going fishing at Didjini.

'All my children and
grandchildren are
good hunters.'

Nancy

Action and connection are two sides of the same coin. People remain in connection with country by being there, and are there responsibly when they are engaged actively with country. The good hunters — *milityin* — are active; they love what they do, and thus do their work with love. Country calls to Mak Mak people, telling them when the fish are biting, the animals are fat, the fruits are ripe and the yams ready to harvest. Each call is a potential. Good hunters turn potentials into realities, and their own lives come into focus and meaning as they answer country's call. Country answers back with food. Thus, the care, nurturance and love continue.

One of the main fishing places for Mak Mak people is the Finniss River near the outstation at Didjini.

Driving the Toyota across the billabong to get to the river.

Bill organising his gear. Bill is Margy's eldest son and Calvin and Rankin's brother.

Margy: Finniss River ~ our fishing spot. That's where the salt water meets the fresh water.

Bill: Two big barra!

Barramundi: (*Lates calcarifer*) is a popular fish with sports-persons and gourmets. Widely distributed in rivers, estuaries and coastal areas of the tropical and sub-tropical regions of the Indo-Pacific, barramundi prefer low-moving or still, muddy waters in rivers, streams, swamps and estuaries. Most fish grow to maturity in the upper reaches of river systems, then migrate downstream with the floodwaters to spawn in estuarine or coastal shallows.[37]

Nancy: I won't starve. I know I'll find good tucker because I have the right sweat for my country.

Good Hunters

'Country gives us our identity. We are created,
live, die and exist in the spirit of all the natural
elements. Our lives are formed in knowing
our country ...'

Linda Ford

KNOWLEDGE

Digging yams in a nearby jungle teaches you the great lesson that ' ... an expert makes things look easy'.[38] Nancy Daiyi walks around in the jungle looking at trees, and eventually she points to the ground and says, 'dig there'. Just after the rains have finished, those who know what they are looking for can see traces of vine stem and flower. Later in the year only a withered string remains to mark the vine, and still the expert knows. How does Nancy know which strings lead to yams, which vines are the most vigorous, and where the best yams will be found? Years of experience count for a lot, as does the fact that she knows these jungles inside out. This is Nancy's country — she has been digging yams here all her life.

In a broader sense, Nancy knows this because the knowledge is hers by right. She and the rest of the Mak Mak people were born into the right to the knowledge of this place: its sacred and dangerous places, resource sites, and the technologies needed to make a living in this country and to take care of it. *Milityin* people combine abstract knowledge of the properties of living things (for example, yam vines look like this, they grow in this way and signal this kind of information) with detailed, concrete knowledge of specific places and information (such as, this jungle is a good place for yams, this time of year is a good time, over there are signs of damage and here the place looks fresh). Their knowledge gives them life; without knowledge, survival would be difficult, perhaps even impossible.

Good hunters don't take everything. They plan to return, and to keep returning. This little jungle contains a history of yam digging: today, it is a site for yams, and it also holds the potential to be a future site for yams. It has nurtured Mak Mak people for generations, and their intentional practice is that the jungle shall continue to do this. They replant stalks, so that the yams will continue to grow.

In contrast to Mak Mak care, local non-Indigenous pastoralists take a far more casual approach to the environment. This jungle is not located on Aboriginal land; it is not being properly burnt with fire breaks, and it is shrinking. Its location is being surveyed for development. It seems that generations of Mak Mak care and nurturance could soon be eradicated if this little relic rainforest disappears.

Margy: There's the Queen Ann (Nancy) perched on a root (right). Full of orders for everyone. Calvin's digging. Don't break off the stem, otherwise it's harder to find the thing.

Nancy watches on while Calvin digs for yams.

Margaret digging for yams.

Kathy: There's Margaret, foraging away there. Persistent as ever.

Linda: And see how she's dug the dirt going down, to make a little seat? To make it comfortable for digging ~ because it takes so long!

Margy: You take all the tucker. It rots if you don't get it all. You put the stalk back.

Kathy: You'd want to eat them really slowly after all that work. You can roast them up, or boil them or roll them in hot coals. But you're not allowed to cut them with a knife or poke them with a fork. When you get them out of the coals, you can get something to beat them, to split them and let the hot air out. We have a special stick called *milityin*. It can't be made from any other tree, only ironwood. Digging stick, made of ironwood. And you call a person *milityin* if they're a really good food gatherer, hunter, good hunter, champion. Like Margaret, and Mum, they're somebody special.

Nancy: And all my grandchildren. *Milityin*: they're happy for that person, 'im got a big mob kangaroo, goanna, porcupine, anything, he bring 'im back.

Margaret with the yam.

JOY IN HUNTING

The joy of hunting is set within the nexus of country and care. People are brought into being by country, and thus are born into relationships of mutuality. As April explained, ' ... if you don't look after country, country won't look after you.' Care and country are mutual.

The other side of this mutuality is that one is taken care of in one's own country. As Nancy said, ' ... when I travel around my country I won't starve. I know I'll find good tucker because I have the right sweat for my country. It'll look after us ... .'

Kathy Deveraux tells a great story:

Kathy: When one of our late uncles was a boy, his father (a master didjeridu player) took him hunting for *muntyirr* (long-neck turtles). His father said, *Ngowana tyabat me, awa muntyirr nala* [that he'd wade around waist or chest deep ~ not the least bit afraid of the numerous crocodiles inhabiting the lagoon ~ and grope around underwater catching as many turtles alive as he could with his bare hands]. Usually when a turtle is caught like this, the hunter will wade across and give it to someone to keep an eye on. If the hunter is alone, the turtles are buried in soft mud on their backs, or placed in a deep hole where they can't climb out, or they're put in a *tupu* [a long, woven, hunting dillybag] ~ designed with a wide band to set across the forehead and carried over the shoulder and down the back.

So, my uncle patiently waited for his father on the bank of this large crocodile-infested lagoon. After a while, the old man decided he'd had enough, and brought his hands up as a sign that he'd been unlucky. That is, a gesture of a blade running across the throat with one deft stroke as if he'd had his throat cut, meaning, 'Well, we're dead, it looks like we'll have to starve'. Then, as he waded into shallower waters, Uncle couldn't believe his eyes. To his delight, his father had caught several *muntyirr* and had tied them by the neck to the tassels of his hair belt. *My fatha bin trien trik mi! Ha maty tharran* [Look how much he got], he laughed, clapping his thighs.[39]

Life's meaning and joy revolve around relationships of care; hunting is a key form of nurturance, and is thus a central activity. When Mak Mak people go hunting, fishing, and getting plant foods, they call out to the country to communicate their presence and their intent. The food they find feeds them and their families, and their practices of care seek to ensure that other living things are also protected and coming into growth. They completely recognise a self-interest in nurturing living things so they will always be available to be hunted, fished or gathered; and this self-interest is central to promoting the continuity of country as a living system.

Margy Daiyi is one of the great hunters, a *milityin* of outstanding accomplishment. She lives at the Didjini 'outstation', a small, family-sized community on a finger of slightly elevated ground that stretches out into the floodplains (see maps pp. xi and xiii). To the west is the boundary hill Ngalgal (Rankin's *mirr* place), and beyond that are the beaches that belong to the coastal peoples (the Wadjigin). Nearby is the swamp called Muluk (Calvin's *mirr* place). To the south stretch the big rivers, floodplains and salt flats. On the east, one follows the Finniss back to its junction with the Florence, and thus back into the high country. Didjini is a Green Ant Dreaming.

Magpie goose: *Anseranas semipalmata* was once found throughout much of Australia, but now the magpie goose is restricted primarily to the monsoonal north. The magpie goose is sufficiently distinct from most other species that some taxonomists think it should be assigned a family of its own. Its most distinctive feature is the absence of full webbing between the toes. For the non-specialist, magpie geese are more commonly known for their distinctive honking than for their unusual toes.[40]

Nancy: Geese. It's tucker. There now, good one!

'Margy Daiyi — somebody special.'

Kathy

RESTRAINT

Good hunters know when to stop hunting. The time to stop hunting geese, for example, is indicated by what the geese have been eating. Good hunters check the goose's throat. Geese prefer to eat a native corm known as onion grass (*Eleocharis dulcis*). When they start eating ordinary grass, Mak Mak people know that tucker for the geese is getting low. When geese begin to lose their preferred tucker, they also lose their good fat condition. Not only are they less preferable as food, but already stressed by their low food supply, they need to be free of other stresses such as being hunted. The exact time to stop hunting geese changes from year to year, depending on a range of variables, with the most critical diagnostic being the goose's tucker.

Mak Mak people's hunting system is ecologically sensitive. The seemingly simple practice of inspecting goose throats accesses numerous variables, including the current rainfall (which affects the condition of the plants that fringe the billabongs), and the goose populations at any given billabong (and thus the pressure they are putting on local resources). Mak Mak people work with this system by hunting when conditions are right, and refraining from hunting when the signs indicate that it is time to stop.

For Mak Mak people, their system is self-regulating. They monitor the geese, and regulate their hunting actions accordingly. There is no coercion here; rather, regulation is part of taking care of the place, doing the right thing and being a good hunter. This is their country, and they are the people who have the responsibility and the right to use it and take care of it. They plan to be here eating geese for generations to come. This point is clear even to a young teenager like Calvin, who asserts:

Calvin: This country is my future, my children's future, my grandchildren after that, and the rest of my family.[41]

Les Waditj and Gary Deveraux bringing in the goose.

Gary Deveraux gutting a goose.

Eggs inside.

Margy holding up the windbag, 'the honker'.

Cooking goose.

Margy: Fat goose. I'm holding up the windbag, the honker. It does make noise, you know. That's his *kenbi* [didjeridu] …

… Oh, you can see, that's the female goose, that one. You can see the eggs. They've got *mutumutu* [eggs] now. They got tiny little eggs inside …

… Goose cooking there.

Good hunters also know how to do things well. This is another reason why people want to be with them: not just to eat well, but to learn well too, and to be certain that things are being done properly. Knowledge lies beneath and informs practice; and action without knowledge can be dangerous.

April: Turtles normally hibernate on the edges of the river system further inland than the banks, or in the billabongs, on the edges of the billabongs or in channel-type areas. Great care must be taken when burning those areas. You don't burn the areas when the turtles are hibernating. We hunt for these turtles by poking in the mud with a crowbar [*nin-nin*], locating them and digging them out of the mud.

'Country tells you' where to go and what to do. Here pandanus trees mark a site where turtles will hibernate during the dry season.

On one occasion we discovered that people had driven out to the area and lit fires, burning the cane grass. We began to hunt for turtles and located a large number. But for each one that we located and went to dig up, all we pulled out was rotting pieces of turtles. The hibernating turtles were cooked and had rotted.

The burning of the cane grass caused the water temperature to become too hot. The fire was lit by people who did not know the country. They did not have any consultation with our people for the country. We call this indiscriminate burning, regardless of what persons they are.[43]

PREDATION

Mak Mak people are hunters, and are enmeshed in predator–prey relationships (predation). Conservationists have often questioned how it can be that people who are ecologically aware, as Indigenous people often seem to be, also have a practice of killing things. The question rests on the false assumption that to love and care for the world around you would prohibit you from wanting to kill

Laurie Waditj.

Laurie Waditj poking for turtles at a site called Kalngarriny.

and eat parts of it. The question appears to equate killing with evil, and thus appears to seek a purity of total abstinence from predation. Mak Mak people do not pose this question; for them, to be alive and to be actively involved is to participate deeply in ecological processes as they exist in the world. They accept both sharing and competition, life and death.

With their cultural fires, Mak Mak people work with the given properties of fire, fire-adapted species, fire-sensitive species and ecosystems. Their work is directed toward enhancing the life-sustaining properties of fire, and minimising its destructive potential. This also enhances their own lives: it makes it easier to see the ground, and to see through the bush; it enables them to organise their harvests; and it attracts animals and facilitates hunting. It is clearly grounded in self-interest. At the same time, this work enhances the lives of other species: it makes it easier for predators (such as lizards) to see and to hunt; and it provides fresh, nutritious growth for herbivores such as kangaroos. Therefore it clearly considers and enhances the interests of others as well. In my experience, Mak Mak people do not seek to think that their actions must be either self-interested or other-interested. In the webs of connection that constitute their world, both kinds of interests are important.

Perhaps because they understand their own lives as part of the life of the country, they do not conceptualise a fundamental opposition between human interests and the interests of other living things. In working with the world (rather than seeking to control or subdue it), self-interest and other-interest co-exist.

Linda: Country gives us our identity. We are created, live, die and exist in the spirit of all the natural elements: night and day, the air, the wind, the water, the plants and animals and the land ... The relationships of each person are connected with the land. Our lives are formed in knowing our country ~ passed down by generations of oral history of the White Eagle people through life and death.[44]

The term 'symbiosis' refers to these kinds of relationships in which living things co-exist with mutual benefit. An example of this is food sharing. Earlier (on p. 29), Nancy told a story about scrounging cycad nuts from emu droppings, and Kathy commented that they were sharing food with emus. They are describing 'commensalism': eating the same foods, or living off the same resources, without excluding others.

not competition?

Billabongs are sites of densely interactive symbiosis. The fact that geese, ducks, brolgas and people all eat *mimirri* [onion grass] shows how the sharing of food creates common interests. All of these creatures have an interest in ensuring an ongoing supply of *mimirri*. The self-interest of organising one's own supply of *mimirri* is balanced by the knowledge that other creatures eat it too, and this interest is not hypothetical. Mak Mak people have waged a long and difficult battle to prevent the invading weed *Mimosa pigra* from taking over the billabong at Didjini and destroying it (pp. 108–117). In keeping the billabong clear, they kept open a habitat rich in vegetable tucker that they and other creatures eat. Consequently, they kept open a site where the animals that come to feed also become prey for Mak Mak hunters.

Mimirri.

Kim Deveraux, Kathy Deveraux's daughter.

Kathy: *Mimirri* tucker. It's *mimirri*. When it dries off it's a little sweet nut in the black soil. Water chestnuts, they're also called. Goose eats it. *Djulburr*. All the ducks eat it too, and brolgas. *Melen* is the Marranunggu word. *Mimirri* is Marrithiel.

Didjini. It's got:

Kathy: Egret (*Egretta intermedia*). *Kunggali*. And that lily there: *ngaram* [right].

Linda: Lilies, with their edible stems and buds, and the stalk can be used as a straw to filter dirty water. The ones with pink flowers, you can eat the bulb. There's the normal billabong weed, and onion grass at the front. Geese eat the corms of the lilies, too. And you hunt for turtle in the lilies and weeds.

Kunggali *(Egret).*

Ngraram *(Lily).*

concepts of race tied to place?

Linda: We use the flowers for our funerals. Like white people use lilies, and we use these lilies. There's medicine here too. The lotus bird hunts here, and magpie geese, whistle ducks, black ducks, miniature ducks, pygmy geese, herons, jabirus, Mak Mak, hawks, gulls even. Swamp harriers, willy wagtails, peewees, plovers. There's barra and sleepy cod, tarpon, catfish in the floodwaters, that's eel tail and fork tail catfish. In the floodwaters there's rifle fish, glass fish, stripeys and crocs, even the Johnston croc might get stranded. And both turtles, short-neck and long-neck. We share the water with all of them, and with the cattle and horses. Everything is there, we all live off the same place. There's snakes and goannas and eels. Everything you want is right there at your fingertips.

Kathy: That's the billabong at night [right]. The large white things are the lilies, and I think those little white things are the frogs' eyes.

Nancy: Lily flowers close at night, did you know that?

Kathy: Yes, do you know why?

Nancy: Because they go to sleep! That's right! Bedtime.

Kathy: Ask a silly question ...

~

From Mak Mak people's perspective, there is no expectation that symbiotic relationships will be devoid of conflict. The daily arguments between a white eagle and a jabiru over fish in the Didjini billabong are a case in point.

Margy: Mak Mak waiting for a feed. The jabiru goes fishing early morning, and the two Mak Mak come in and poach the fish off the jabiru, and they have a big barney [argument] over the fish. The jabiru runs at them with his wings flapping. One takes off, drops the fish, and the jabiru will grab it. And the other Mak Mak will come in and grab it, and they'll spend half the morning fighting over the fish. The jabiru ends up winning, because he takes it into the water and the Mak Maks can't get it.

Mak Mak waiting for a feed.

Didjini billabong at night (right).

Banyan: (*Ficus virens var. virens*) is a tree that can grow to an enormous size; they produce large aerial and prop roots. They grow in monsoonal vine thickets (jungles) in coastal and escarpment areas.

Linda net-fishing at Didjini.

Linda: A long time ago Mum learned to throw the net. Olden times, they used to have a net, those old people. They used to make it with *binbin*, or with banyan tree vines [*Ficus virens*]. Used to weave it out of that one. *Binbin* is a long skinny bamboo that only grows in certain places.

To live in the world, to take care of the world, to find joy and humour in the life of the world is to live symbiotically with it. To be brought into being by it, intimately connected with it, nurtured by it, and to return to it at death, means participating: taking as well as giving, being fed as well as enhancing the life of the place. Nothing in this world view says that predation is wrong, only that it is not to be undertaken without knowledge and care.

The interactions between humans and crocodiles reveal some of the problems of predation from a human perspective, for it is only in this relationship that Mak Mak people are likely prey. Mak Mak people do not ordinarily kill and eat the large, salt water 'man-eating' crocodiles (although some of the men from time to time worked as croc shooters when this was a viable business). Their expectation is that crocs will not eat them. According to Nancy, if a person went missing and the group concluded that a croc had taken them, people would go and call out to the croc. 'Did you get that person?' they would ask. And they would tell the croc to return the body. 'Bring him back to me,' they would say. They would keep calling to the croc to bring the body back to the edge of the river or billabong, and then they would kill the croc, and roast and eat it.[45]

Sometimes when Mak Mak people go fishing at the billabongs that are densely populated by crocodiles, they call out to the crocodiles to persuade them to show themselves. Once the people know where the crocs are, they go to another section of the billabong to fish. No one wants to be prey. As Kathy said, ' ... a *militiyin* has to out-think and out-smart them all.'

Linda: We talk to the crocodiles, and Mum can make a crocodile come up. The big ones are 15 feet plus, and she talks to them and she brings them up. I've tried it, but I can only bring the little ones up.

Kathy: We used to stand in the shallows up there and cast, because the floodwaters used to flatten the onion grass, and you could see the barras chomping in between the onion grass for little frogs. And we used to get in there with our rods. And swim the channel to get from one side to the other and follow the channel down toward Didjini.

Linda calls to crocodiles at PatjPatj billabong.

Kathy: Oh, there's a 'gator (above). That's at Mowzie, where we used to camp and go fishing.

Kathy: Margaret was with Mum one day at this place. And Mum wanted to go fishing on the other side of the channel with Margaret. Mum got tired, and she said, 'I got a good idea, you throw the rope across and tow me across. Youse take off in the jeep and pull me over real quick!'

Colin: Just like a lure! (Colin is Margy's husband.)

Linda: And we used to swim across with our lines, and the babies on our backs, to go down toward Didjini and fish along the channel. In some areas it's pretty wide.

Kathy: We would be fishing in the water, standing in the water up to our knees, and the kids just diving around, swimming. We'd spend the whole day or weekend up there, just getting in amongst the barra. Not even worrying about the crocs. Couldn't care less.

White-breasted sea-eagle: (*Haliaetus leucogaster*), often described as 'magnificent', and 'splendid', is a maritime bird of prey with a two-metre wing span. It rides the thermals along the estuaries and inland waterways, or perches on dead trees watching for prey. For preference it swoops on fish, flying foxes, pythons, waterfowl and turtles.[46]

Linda: Well, how come they never ate us?

Kathy: Because they had plenty of barra!

Mak Mak people share a way of life with other predators; they all live off many of the same foods. The white-breasted sea-eagle [Mak Mak] is the most prominent of these other predators with which Mak Mak people share a way of life. The people are good hunters, and so are the birds; and they share many of the same foods.

Kathy: He's going hunting. When the wings are like that, he's coming down for landing. He's on the lookout here. When he's flying like that, he's looking for feed.

Leaves are used to stop the liver and eggs from popping out.

Margy holding a short-neck turtle — the short-neck turtle is Richard's mirr.

Margy: This is the short-neck turtle. Mak Mak eat them, we eat them too.

Margy: The leaves are to stop the liver and eggs from popping out while the turtle's cooking, and to keep the juices in. With the short-neck turtle, you can't pull the guts out from the neck because the neck's so short. The gut is different to the long-neck turtle. The short-neck turtle's gut is shorter than the long-neck's. We just crack the sides. It's easier to get the gut from the side of the short-neck turtle. You know, the short-neck turtle is Richard's *mirr*.

KINSHIP WITH ANIMALS

Anthropologists generally use the term 'totemism' to describe structured relationships between human groups and 'natural' species. Totems are about connection; the relationship is of profound and enduring significance. These connections between humans and animal and plant species, or with other parts of the natural world, overlap and crosscut each other. Not only is every person in connection totemically, but equally significantly, they are in connection with numerous species. The different ways of being connected produce for each person a web of kinship with the natural world. The white-breasted sea-eagle is the clan totem: this is the Mak Mak clan. The people are connected to each other, to sea-eagles and to the sites of sea-eagle significance.

Mak Mak, the clan totem (right).

Mak Mak coming down to land.

April: This place here [right], when we look at this hill, it's the heartbeat of this country. From here we look ~ we look straightaway and we know this is the White Eagle place here, and we feel really deeply because this is where all our language come from, handed down from the White Eagle, and all our ceremonies.

This was Mum's favourite place here. She used to come here all the time. She took all the kids. Anybody that was travelling with her always came past here ... In our heart, from long time, all our Dreaming stories, no matter white man got fence lines everywhere, they cut this country up. Aboriginal way, our way, that country goes right past Dreaming tracks, and you can't cut it off with fence lines.[47]

Linda: Kalngarriny. Mak Mak hill. That's the Dreaming place for Mak Mak.

White stones: that's eagle's turd. White eagle's droppings, droppings cooked in the sun.

Mak Mak Hill (Dreaming place for Mak Mak).

Totemic relationships that define groups are reproduced in regular and predictable ways from generation to generation; they are quite unlike *mirr*, the individual's Dreaming, which connects people unpredictably. The white-breasted sea-eagle is the Dreaming or totem that identifies this clan, and differentiates it from other Marranunggu clans:

Linda: Our clan totem is the Mak Mak, the white-bellied sea-eagle. The Mak Mak gives us our language and law to the country we belong to. Our *ngirrwat* [totem/Dreaming] gives us our kinship system.

Our kinship system is divided into two. For example, my grandmother's *ngirrwat* are *migut* [dingo] and *panypiyatuk* [possum]. My grandfather's *ngirrwat* are the Mak Mak and *ngarran* [goanna].[48]

Kathy: Creatures great and small are our *ngirrwats*. Fire is a *ngirrwat*, trees are a *ngirrwat*. *Ngirrwats* are also part of the kinship system. The white sea-eagle is my mother's father. We relate to it as our grandfather...[49]

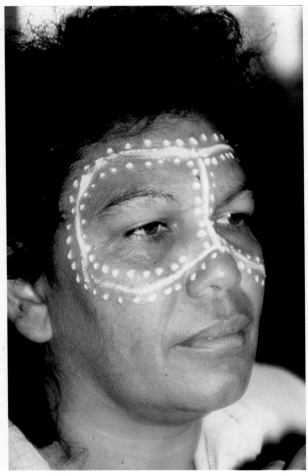

Kathy Deveraux. (Photo by D Rose)

'When you put the
white paint on your
face ... you just make
it like ... it's hood.'

Kathy

Nancy: That eagle belongs to Marranunggu language. Marranunggu Dreaming. Mak Mak. *Ngirrwat*. That's my Dreaming. Mak Mak. White Eagle. Poor bugger, my Dreaming. White Eagle.

Kathy: White Eagle, you call it Daddy.

When you put the white paint on your face, you just make it like ~ that way. Like it's hood, you follow that forehead round, back up under the eye here, under the cheek.

Mak Mak, the white-breasted sea-eagle (Nancy's Daddy).

Stringybark tree.

'This tree here, we call
"uncle" this tree.'

Nancy

Kathy: Stringybark is for the women, and woolybutt is for the men. They call it 'uncle'. So, we're not just related to *ngirrwat* for animals. We've got relationships to trees. That's Mum's uncle, stringybark.

Nancy: You too.

Kathy: Like White Eagle, you call it Daddy.

The totemic or *ngirrwat* system includes clan totems, gender totems, lineage totems and more. Their complexity, along with the intensity of connection, draws people into empathetic and respectful relations with their world.

Migut *(Dingo)*.

Dingo: (*Canis lupus*) is a recent arrival to Australia. On current evidence, it has been in Australia for the past 3500 years. The dingo is the living representative of ancestral canines. Once they ranged across much of the world, but selective breeding under domestication meant that most dog breeds today are highly diverse, and only the Australian dingo and its counterparts in Papua New Guinea, Asia, and a few parts of Africa remain similar to the ancestral dog.[50]

Linda: Dingo — that's us. *Migut*. The dingo.

Margy: This one is my Dreaming.

Nancy: This one is my mother.

Kathy, Margy, Linda and their brother Richard are Mak Mak Dreaming from their mother's father. In addition, they are Dingo *ngirrwat* (totem/Dreaming) from their mother's mother. When we saw a dingo in the bush one day and stopped to take photos, Margy and Linda whistled to catch its attention. They whistled in unison, replicating exactly the scale and harmonics of dingoes howling at night.

There is no way to explain the sound of dingoes howling. If you have heard coyotes or wolves, you can imagine what it is like. Could you imagine two women whistling like dingoes? You know how you feel when your skin goes cold and your hair stands on end? Dingo women do this to you without even trying.

Kathy: Creatures great and small are our ngirrwats.

Tracks and Lives

'Most everything ... like the fencing, yards and
stock in here, it's all been like family effort. What
has been put here, we put here out of our
pockets and with our own effort.'

Richard Daiyi

BELONGING

Country is the place of belonging. The people, the other living things, the waters and soils, rains and winds all bring each other into being, nurturing and impacting on each other. Linear models of cause and effect are too simple to describe the dynamic, symbiotic, kinship-based, mutually nurturant and sometimes predatory relationships between people, non-human beings and place. What happens to one affects what happens to another; but most importantly, all have long-term commitments to these relationships that nurture their lives. Mak Mak people expect to remain in their country 'forever'. Accordingly, changes in the place, even the most damaging, must be lived with. There are no 'greener pastures' for them, because they belong right here.

Archaeologists working with the best evidence available at this time estimate that Aboriginal people have been in Australia for at least 60 000 years. During this time there were major environmental changes that, in the Wagait region, were experienced primarily as rising and falling sea levels, and varying patterns of rainfall. Geologically speaking, the Wagait floodplains are a recent ecosystem. Ten thousand years ago the sea was much lower than it is now, and the Wagait area was a much drier place. When the seas rose, the Wagait was inundated with salt water. About 6000 years ago the sea stabilised, and the Wagait became a huge mangrove swamp. Even more recently, within the past 4000 years, the salt swamps have become the rich, fresh water systems they are today. The floodplains are so flat, and the rain so intensely seasonal, that the big rivers are unusually dynamic. Billabongs, old river beds and gigantic meanders testify to the mobility of the rivers. Studies of aerial photographs of the nearby Daly River show the river bed to be in a continuing state of change.[51] Undoubtedly there have been many human adaptations to these changes, and it seems probable that much of the social change is subsumed within a philosophy of 'time immemorial'.

COLONISATION

British occupation of the continent began in 1788, when the first settlers arrived to found a penal colony. Across Australia, decade by decade, massacres, diseases, malnutrition, starvation, dispersal and assimilation were used to force Indigenous peoples from their homelands and their bases of subsistence. People were killed or concentrated in reserves, missions, cattle properties or fringe camps. Many were forced into settlements, others took refuge with settlers as protection against other settlers and government policies.

Official and unofficial government policy and practice aimed to manage the elimination of Indigenous people. In an earlier period, physical dispossession and disease accomplished this. Subsequently, widespread and massive damage to families and individuals was inflicted under a policy of assimilation which proposed to absorb Aborigines into 'white' society. This policy authorised many forms of what we now call 'cultural cleansing'.[52] For example, it enabled missionaries to raise children in dormitories, away from their families, in the interests of 'civilising' them. Until 1967 Aboriginal people were not counted in the national census. They were legally not citizens, but rather wards of the state, and were denied fundamental human rights. In the early 1970s the federal government adopted an official policy of self-determination for Aboriginal people. As of June 2010 the population of Australia was about 22, 342,400 people. Aboriginal people comprised about 2.5 per cent of that number. In the Northern Territory where the proportion of Aboriginal population is greater than elsewhere, Aboriginal people constitute 30 per cent of the population.[53]

From about the 1860s, the Darwin hinterland was occupied by settlers from a variety of cultural origins: there were Macassan traders who came to gather the sea slug known as *trepang*, as well as other international traders, administrators and surveyors; small-scale miners, both European and Chinese, as well as large-scale mining ventures; telegraph operators and government drillers, agriculturalists, pastoralists and buffalo shooters; Chinese traders, plantation owners and managers, commercial fishermen and croc shooters; and explorers, naturalists, police, drifters, missionaries and other adventurers with a variety of motivations. Aboriginal people had access not only to the standard tobacco, flour, sugar and tea, but also to alcohol and opium. They also had access to many sets of international ideas and ideals, to opportunities to play the different groups off against each other, and to sample for themselves a range of ways of living.

Prior to 1911, the Northern Territory was classified as part of South Australia, and was administered under a system of land use that specifically required the creation of reserves where Aboriginal people could continue to live in their own way. The Wagait was reserved for Aboriginal people in 1892 (re-gazetted in 1911),[54] but, contrary to what one might expect, Aboriginal people did not enjoy untrammelled security on their own reserve land. The land itself was also occupied by a range of white settlers: there were miners, timber-getters, croc shooters and others. The owners of adjacent cattle properties held grazing leases over the reserve. In effect, the reserve became part of the neighbouring properties:

Kathy: Our European father is an Australian-born Canadian. His name is Max Sargent. He was part of the Sargent family. They had 14 in their family, and they pioneered this country. They've got a house that they built on Blyth homestead in the Litchfield Park [now a tourist site] ... My father's father, old Harry, he had a lot of country leases, or whatever, grazing licences. Dad owned ... Finniss River [station], which used to be called Roslyn Plain, and we've been on this land all the time with him, with my mother, with her family.

We've been mustering here on horseback. I was born here. He carried me in his shirt on his horse, and I grew up here with him in the stock camps and with my Marranunggu family and my Marrithiel family. That's who he had working for him at the time.[55]

In the early years of colonisation, people in the Wagait area sought protection from massacres, from men who stole women, and from a variety of enforced labour relations. They also sought positive relationships with white settlers, and continued to flee negative relationships.[56] In the subsequent decades, protection was also sought against Australia's assimilation policy, which authorised the forcible removal from their families of children of mixed ancestry.[57] April's family tried to protect her, and in the end they agreed to allow her to go away for institutionalised education:

April: I was born up here at the old tin mine. I was born in the sweet potato patch from that garden, and my other cousins was born here too. This place here has Dreaming too for *yanginmarra*, and that word means mermaids.

Next year I'm 50. And that welfare mob come out here and they took us away, we was only little baby ... But before that my grandmother Wulmarra, she used to run away with us on top of the hill ... She used to run away up the hill, and she used to roll rocks down so they didn't get us. But they did end up getting us with agreeance to our father that we be educated at Croker Island. We was put out at Croker Island and we used to come home for holidays. We were the only family that come back to country for a holiday ... And they used to come out and visit us at Croker Island. They knew all them kids there now, they were starving for mummy, too, they used to call out, 'Mum, Mum'.[58]

Kathy, Margy and Richard were born in the bush, and their existence was concealed from the authorities who would have institutionalised them. Linda was grabbed, but Nancy defied the authorities, and Max Sargent, the father, went to court to keep his Aboriginal family together:

Nancy Daiyi.

'Mum and I ran away to her tribal country.'

Linda

Linda: In the 1960s, my father owned two properties where my mother and her family relations could stay together as an extended family clan to work on the properties. I was born in a small town hospital at Batchelor, Northern Territory. Mum and I were driven from Batchelor Hospital to the Darwin Royal Hospital. When Mum was stronger, the welfare officers ordered us to go to the Bagot Native Reserve. Mum was instructed that she had to wait there until the welfare officers came to talk to her about her 'half-caste' baby. However, Mum had other plans.

Mum and I ran away to her tribal country, Kurrintyu [Kurrindju]. We made it to the stock camp at Karkar, where Dad was working with Tyabuty Tyarrabuty [grandfather Tjarrabutj (Tjarrabak), Green Ant Paddy [see Genealogical Sketch, p. xii], and other family on the new set of stock yards. The local police officer came for us. Dad was summoned to appear in court at Darwin. The outcome: Dad and his first wife, also a non-Indigenous person, were ordered to become our custodians. In so far as this reflected the treatment of Indigenous Australians this was a sad event, but it was also empowering because our family's Mak Mak pedagogical practices were consolidated. We were able to maintain our family unit which constitutes our local descent group and which is significant to learning about caring for country.[59]

The yard they were building when Nancy and the infant Linda made it back from town was named 'Linda's Yard'. This became a new place of significance: a site where Linda was saved for her family, and where Nancy Daiyi and Max Sargent took a stand against the Australian government.

Many sites fix and hold these entangled webs of coercion, resistance, love and hurt. Another such site is Abijak, the hill near where Nancy was born. Her family was working with miners at the tin mines near there at the time of her birth.

Kathy: That's Mum's birth place (below). To the left are the headwaters for the Florence, and the dark hill to the right is Abijak and Makanba.

Tin mine.

We asked Mines and Energy to rehabilitate, but they wouldn't rehabilitate because, something about getting the land back.

And they were mining uranium at Rum Jungle near Batchelor, and all the acids and heavy metal ran down the East Finniss branch, poisoning all the trees and fish. That's the branch that runs into the Florence junction, where the Goose was walking along blowing his *kenbi*.

Nancy's birth place.

STATUS OF THE LAND

Within the Northern Territory, the *Aboriginal Land Rights (NT) Act 1976 (C'wth)* gave a legal basis to the possibility of secure land tenure. Under this legislation, the many reserves of the Territory that had already been set aside for Aboriginal people's use automatically came under Aboriginal Freehold Title without having to go through a claim procedure. The Land Rights Act contained the provision that matters concerning Aboriginal land would be handled by Land Councils, which were formed as statutory bodies under the Act.

One of the Land Councils' first tasks was to determine the traditional owners of reserve lands, so that a register of owners could be compiled; then, anyone who needed to consult with traditional owners would know who the right people were. The Northern Land Council twice decided that Mak Mak people were not the traditional owners of the reserve itself. There is a long and hurtful history surrounding the question of ownership that can be summarised by saying that during the years 1976–1994, traditional ownership of the Wagait was contested.

April Bright spoke of the old people's distress in this period, when it looked like they might be legally dispossessed:

April: That [Land Council action] was putting them right under, because these people, they know their law. They know their Dreamings, and that law, blackfella law, belong to that country. Without country you got no law. Those two go together. You got country, you got law. And Mum and Uncle, they was really worried for that, because that was putting them right under. They might as well have dug a hole and buried people right there and then, because they were the people that ruled this country, the old people, and they wasn't allowed to do that. So to them, they got knocked down to the status of being *pigipigi* [feral pigs] … [60]

Don't get me misunderstood. Us Marranunggu, we don't lose country. No matter we might be somewhere else because somebody else is on this country. To us this country's still ours and will always be. [61]

Margy and others took the Northern Land Council to court, charging that the Mak Mak people had not been given a fair hearing. [62] In 1992, the Northern Land Council decided to try to bring the matter to resolution by conducting a formal investigation in which each group would have the assistance of an anthropologist and a lawyer in presenting their claim to a specially appointed panel.

The Mak Mak people's search for an anthropologist brought us together and enabled us to form the friendships that make this book possible. During

The Mak Mak clan and associates at Fred's Pass, Darwin, February 1994, prior to a day giving evidence before the Wagait Committee. Standing (left to right): Dominic Toomey, Mark Ford, Linda Ford, Margaret Waditj, Pavalina Nickaloff, Kathy Deveraux, Colin Deveraux, Kim Deveraux, Annie Bright, Richard Daiyi, April Bright, Ziggy; in the Jungle Jim (left to right): Laurie Waditj, Andy Belyuen, John Waditj; seated in front (left to right): Margy Daiyi, Nancy Daiyi, Debbie Rose, Rusty Waditj. (Photo by D. Lewis)

most of 1993 we prepared the documentation for their case, and in late 1993 we were joined by the lawyer, Dominic Toomey. Together we took the case before the panel in a formal hearing that first convened on the land, and later re-convened in town. The result of this arduous process was that the panel determined that the Mak Mak people were the traditional owners of much (but not all) of the land they claimed. With renewed security of title, they are now able to recuperate some of the clan's coherence, and to resume unambiguous control of the social and environmental factors that enable them to care for their country.

Kathy: White Eagle Aboriginal Corporation is a registered organisation which services the needs and aspirations of its members, who are of the 'Rak Mak Mak Marranunggu' clan and their beneficiaries. Other than providing opportunities for better health, housing, education and training and an economic base in the cattle industry, it has taken on board a program to strategically manage and control further outbreaks of mimosa to reclaim our cultural sites of significance.[63]

Hearing at Kalngarriny, the 'heartbeat of the country'. Nancy Daiyi is giving evidence. She wears body paint and is rubbed in red ochre. Behind her is the Banyan tree at Kalngarriny. (Photo by D. Lewis)

These emplaced events and stories show the interconnection between the lives of the people, the history and geography of the place, and the colonising and decolonising relations that have entangled them all.

Wherever you go in Mak Mak country, there are stories. The stories are situated in place, and there are signs like trees or yards that mark the place. These marks are histories, and they include histories of violence and damage, of determination and struggle, along with care and nurturance. The old and the new co-exist, and the bittersweet entanglements of place shape the lives of people who intend to remain there 'forever'.

CATTLE

Now that Mak Mak people enjoy security of tenure, they can engage in their own economic ventures. One of these is agistment of cattle; the proceeds from this are mainly used to pay for programs to control the invasive weed *Mimosa pigra*, for which government funding is insufficient. One can recognise a vicious circle here in which an invasive species with one set of impacts (cattle) is used to bring in cash to fund the control of another invasive species (mimosa). Unlike ferals, however, cattle are highly controlled, and the impacts can be monitored and managed. In addition, cattle have been a part of Mak Mak culture for decades. As Kathy said, she was born in a stock camp and spent her early years on her Dad's horse. The involvement of the whole clan, their organisation of labour, their ability to use their knowledge and skills to bring in a cash income and their dedication to herd management are all significant parts of people's lives. The agistment enterprise fattens cattle for overseas export. The enormous amounts of nutritious grass, and the proximity to the live export industry in Darwin make the Wagait a desirable agistment area.

The Daiyi herd is kept at Didjini. Every year the cattle are mustered, branded and de-horned. Some are destined for the meatworks, others are turned back onto the land to graze for another year. Richard Daiyi explains:

Richard: Most everything what's been put here, like the fencing, yards and stock in here, it's all been like family effort. Everyone comes here and puts into it. What has been put here, we put here out of our pockets and with our own effort. We've got about 220 head, and they have been tested. They're TB-free, and we yard them up say three times a year just to get them used to the yards, get them used to people and keep them quiet, and the only way to keep stock is to keep them quiet. Then you can walk around them, and they're not galloping over everything and breaking through your fences.[64]

Richard Daiyi. Richard is Kathy, Linda and Margy's brother.

Rankin and his father, Gary Deveraux Snr (Kathy's husband), start the muster [round-up].

Pastoral Industry: The first European explorers of North Australia had a keen eye for pasture land, and between 1860 and 1890 much of the land in what was to become the Northern Territory was divided into pastoral leases, at least on paper. Until the late 1960s the predominant breed of cattle was the Shorthorn, but since that time pastoralists have been shifting their herds toward Brahman breeds that are better suited to the tropics.[65]

Rankin, Gary and Colin in the yards getting the cattle ready for branding.

Les, a Wagait
cattleman.

Les brands a calf.

Rankin castrates a calf.

In the yard.

Calvin in the yard.

Margy carries a young calf to the truck.

In a moment of rest, Kim sprays the horse.

FERALS

Colonisation brought a series of biological invasions. The water buffalo is a good example. Introduced to the Northern Territory on numerous occasions from the 1830s on, buffalo were well-adapted to the tropical floodplains and they flourished. By 1981 the Wagait had the highest concentrations of buffalo in the whole of Australia's monsoonal lowlands.[66]

Scientific study of the impacts of buffalo began in the 1970s;[67] and one scientist's statement sums up (in lay terms) a multitude of effects: ' ... it was a real environmental crash, a spectacular disaster.'[68] As Mak Mak people have explained to me, and as scientifically-trained ecologists also state, the activities of buffalo create loss of ground cover and loss of water plants; soil erosion, compaction and pollution of waterholes are increased;[69] floating grass mats are broken up, with resulting loss of major breeding habitats;[70] and there is increased fresh water run-off, siltation and tidal influence. Buffalo are responsible for drastic reductions in jungles. In addition, as buffalo slither along levee banks they break the banks down and create deep channels, enabling intrusion of salt water and subsequent paperbark die back.[71]

During the decades of buffalo invasion, the Wagait floodplains were heavily grazed and an extensive network of tracks was formed. Swamps and billabongs showed severe reduction of vegetative cover on the banks, severe reduction of grass mats and areas of bank erosion. By 1980 or so, the salt water intrusion had caused 300 hectares of paperbark die back, extensive death of fresh water grasses and was threatening the lower fresh water section of the Finniss River (particularly the area of Bulkany — see map, p. xiii).[72]

Mak Mak people have personally witnessed the buffalo damage, the salt intrusions, the erosion and build-up of silt. Along with these changes, they saw changes in the country's resources. As they have explained to me, and as specialists also assert, buffalo are linked to the disappearance of red water lilies, the reduction in canegrass (Phragmites) and bullrushes (amongst others), and massive declines in numbers of magpie geese.[73] In addition to the loss of paperbark swamps, buffalo are also linked to the loss of jungle patches. While some of these plants and animals — red lilies and magpie geese in particular — are known to recover,[74] jungles are far more fragile and are unlikely to re-establish themselves.[75]

By the mid-1980s it was clear that a concerted effort to eradicate feral bovines would be necessary for the controlled herds to be freed of tuberculosis and brucellosis. The Wagait was an area in which wholesale slaughter of beasts was trialled, and some 35 000 buffalo and cattle were killed there in the interests of disease eradication.[76]

BTEC: In 1970 the Australian government initiated the Brucellosis and Tuberculosis Eradication Campaign to clean up all Australian herds in order to bring meat exports up to world standards. North Australia posed particular difficulties, and costs of disease eradiation were correspondingly high. The campaign offered the opportunity to eliminate feral bovines across much of the north. Cattle were eradicated where they could not be controlled, and compensation was paid to pastoral lessees.[77]

Feral pigs: The pig (*Sus scrofa*) population in North Australia is probably descended from a range of Asian and European ancestors. They were reported to be common in the wetlands by the 1920s. The expanding pig population is kept in check by the fact that there is an export market for Australian wild pig.[78]

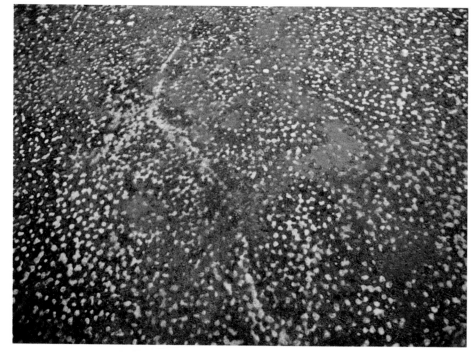

Margy: Pig holes out on the flat. Holy Hell. Death to all pigs!

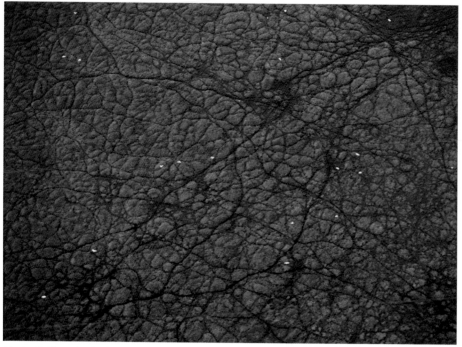

Linda: Bulkany basin. And pig tracks. Water underneath, and that's all the spoonbills flying across.

Banyan tree at Kalngarriny. This is the Mak Mak tree and site that appears in the picture of Nancy Daiyi giving evidence on p. 99, and earlier on p. 85.

Buffalo: The Asian water buffalo (*Bubalus bubalis*) was brought to North Australia from Timor and other parts of what is now Indonesia in the first half of the nineteenth century. The greatest concentrations remained within 100 kilometres of the coast. In 1981 the highest concentrations of buffalo were in the region of the Finniss and Reynolds Rivers.[79] Since that time, the BTEC campaign has almost eliminated buffalo, except under controlled supervision.

Colin: Look at all the buffalo track around the tree. That ring, where the trunk is worn, that's from buffalo. Buffalo and bullocky, mostly buffalo. They stay in the shade all day polishing their horns up.

Margy: That's our Mak Mak tree (above).

Since the feral buffalo have been effectively removed, some portions of the country have made a remarkable recovery, and a few diminished species are now themselves increasers. For example, cane grass — once heavily impacted by buffalo — is now recuperating at the expense of other native grasses.

The impacts of buffalo are emblematic of similar impacts by other ferals. Pigs tear up the country and compete with native animals for certain foods, but the full extent of the damage they cause is still unknown. Evidence suggests that pig populations are low where buffalo populations are high, and since the eradication of the feral buffalo, there has been an explosion of the pig population.

MIMOSA

The most serious and devastating contemporary change is the invasion of *Mimosa pigra*, a woody weed that thrives in wet ground. In surprisingly short periods of time, mimosa blocks waterways, thus radically altering the capacity of the wetlands to nurture a diversity of species. The disturbances caused by buffalo facilitated conditions that now favour the invasion of this noxious weed. It is possible that buffalo helped keep mimosa under control even as they facilitated its subsequent spread.[80]

Kathy: That's all the different shades of water [bottom]. There's mimosa, and para grass. The dark green, that's the mimosa, on the edge of the dry ground. The brown is ridge country. Rice grass, para grass, cane grass. Cane grass is all the little brown bits. It's everywhere. They're walking everywhere now [increasing like mad], that cane grass.

Colin: All this floodplain used to be covered in cane grass. Them old men used to come round, and young men, for fighting spear ~ and they used to cut that cane grass for fighting spear.[81]

Mimosa pigra: A native of South America, *Mimosa pigra* is a woody shrub with prickles. It was introduced to Australia as an ornamental and has since gone wild, taking over vast areas of floodplains and swamps, converting them to shrublands. Loss to native flora and fauna is extreme. The shrubs reproduce rapidly, and follow the waterways, with the potential to damage severely large portions of the northern wetlands and river systems.[82]

Mimosa (dark green) on the edge of the dry ground.

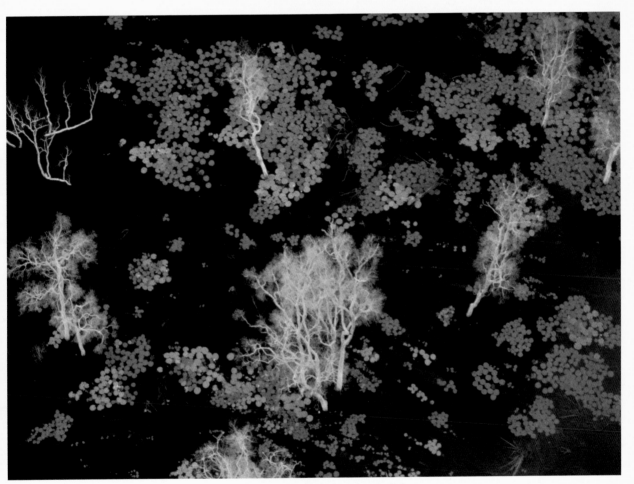

Kathy: Dead paperbark. That's salt water intrusion, probably caused by buffalo.

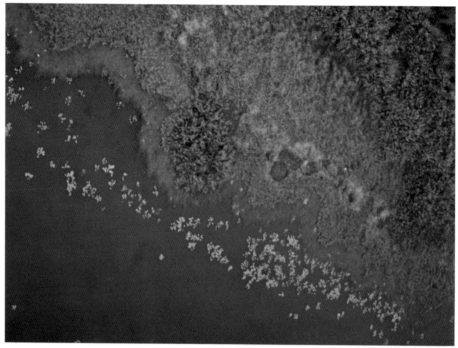

Mimosa on the floating grass.

Linda: You can see mimosa on the floating grass. There is cabbage grass, and floating grass, and that's mimosa there too.

This invasion went out of control on the Wagait during the period in which ownership of the land was being contested. The changes wrought are vast and complex, and strategies for control are still being devised and debated. Billabongs are shrinking, vegetation is changing and habitats are being lost. On the flood-plains and along the water, mimosa grows into impenetrable blocks of thorny thickets. In blocking the waterways and destroying the billabongs, mimosa has the potential to turn the Mak Mak people's home into a wasteland. In addition, mimosa increases the fuel load, so that any accidental fire can become a devastation. Potentially, the country sustained for millennia through human knowledge and care could be reworked into a totally different ecosystem in a matter of decades. The urgency of the issues is thus unmistakable. Laurie Waditj said, 'it makes me feel sick inside just to look at it'.

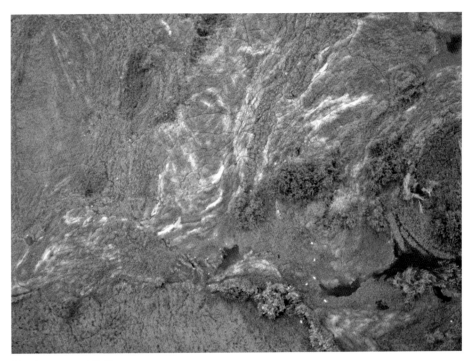

Floating grass at Bulkany.

Kathy: That's floating grass at Bulkany. There's waves and waves of grass. It looked like someone had raked it all up and stacked it in big wrinkles right across the whole landscape. Masses and masses, all compressing at one end. It can't get out. It's choking up. Everything, mimosa, paperbark.

Margy: Why it's in waves is because the mimosa is blocking the passage of all the stuff that's coming down in the floods. It's not flushing.

And there's actually paperbark trees and mimosa growing on top of the billabongs, so they're getting smaller. Like, PatjPatj billabong has shortened up by a half kilometre, because the mimosa's stopping it from flushing. Now Bulkany billabong is only two and a half metres deep. Before, it was four or five metres.

The little fine lines like wrinkles are made from pig tracks. The brown is the grass that's been pushed up from the floods. The blue at the top is the billabong. We saw pigs there, and they ran under the scrub there to hide.

Margy: A mimosa island that floats up and down at Bulkany. A mimosa island that floats. It's mimosa on a mat of floating grass.

Linda: Look at that mimosa in amongst the paperbark (right). When the fire comes through in the Dry it burns that mimosa real hot, and kills the paperbark.

During the years when ownership of the Wagait was officially in limbo, Mak Mak people kept mimosa out of the home billabong at Didjini by relentlessly bulldozing the plants and burning them. Once secure title was regained, they became eligible to apply for Commonwealth and Territory funds, and thus to implement a more intensive program of mimosa control. Biological controls are used as long-term measures, and herbicides are sprayed from helicopters as short-term measures:

Colin: Formerly there was no mimosa here. It was all level, flat country right around, and the mimosa came and cut off all these waterholes right through, and we actually had a little walkway here for the pump to get through it ~ just nearly had a point where we couldn't get through it. We got an old bucket tractor and nearly killed it clearing a hole and just pushing mimosa all out the

Mimosa in amongst the paperbark.

Kim and Colin Deveraux planting grass to take over from dead mimosa. Behind them is a solid wall of dying mimosa.

back. And two and one half year ago we got a little bulldozer and started getting ahead and pushed all this. The mimosa there was a thick wall here, right up to the fence. We pushed it back, burnt it all up. You can still see bits of stick and that along the edge, and we got para grass runners here, on the other side, and ploughed it all up and planted it, put this little fence here to keep the cattle out while it comes. It crawls, that grass, and takes it over, and makes a big mat where the mimosa can't get through. And before, when that mimosa completely encased these waterholes here, there was no geese. They couldn't walk around. And since we've cleared it, you can see how many have come back, big mob. It's like it was before, before the mimosa was here ... If we see one little bit of mimosa come up in there, we get the spray and a biodegradable poison and knock it back, and there's no seed left in that part. It's all covered up with the mat of grass.[83]

Kathy: We've travelled through dead mimosa. And in some areas we travel through in big burrows or tunnels, with four-wheel drive trucks. That's how high the mimosa can grow, over a tray-back Toyota.

This photo was taken in 1993 when there was no funding for mimosa control. Mak Mak people attempted to keep an area of the home billabong clear so that they could still have a place for geese and fish. The dark green on the other side of the billabong is mimosa. You can see several bands of it: one along the edge of the billabong, one behind that, and one stretching back beyond the paperbark trees. (Photo by D. Rose)

This 1997 photo shows the effect of government assistance on mimosa control. The mimosa that formerly was on the edge of the billabong is now gone; the mimosa behind it is dead; and the farthest band remains.

Mimosa growing on top of Bulkany billabong.

Margy: All the green on top, that's mimosa growing on top of Bulkany. It used to be billabong, now it's mimosa. And that's another little island that comes up to the Leichhardt tree. A mimosa island that floats up and down. Mimosa on a floating mat.

Linda: And you can see where that big fire came in from the coast. It came around Mowzie side and burned for two months there. It came right around all the *memeken* [floating grass] and along the high ground, and burnt all that part there, look. On the right-hand side.

This part here, this used to be water all the way around here. And now the water can't go anywhere, because of the mimosa blocking that now. Everything's just growing and taking over on top of the floating mats.

Margy: And since we got it back, we've made that into a paddock, the money that we get from the agistment of cattle goes back into treating the mimosa.

Linda: All on that left-hand side of the billabong there has been treated with chemicals. And all the stuff on the right-hand side is left for bio-control.

At the bottom of Bulkany we saw pigs walking on the floating grass.

We used to get 40-pound barra there. It was good clean water all the way down.

Good clean water at Didjini (right).

WHERE THE RAINBOW DIED

The billabong and swamp known as Bulkany hold many signs and memories: Dreaming action, histories of daily life, and evidence of some of the massive changes that have occurred in recent years with the invasions of habitat-destroying weeds and feral animals.

In creation, this place was made by the Rainbow Snake. Remember how Old Man Goose called all the animals in for a ceremony at Djulurrk billabong? The Rainbow Snake came too, and later he stole the fire and tried to take it to the sea and drown it. As he twisted and turned his way across the land trying to find the sea, he scarred the land. The huge tracks of his struggle to break through to the salt water are there today (see Map of Mak Mak Dreamings, p. xiii). Eventually he turned around and came back to Bulkany billabong, and there he died.

Bulkany is a place where all kinds of living things find their sustenance. It is a prime place for nesting crocodiles, and a great place for Mak Mak hunters. This place also stands in dire jeopardy from mimosa.

Colin: Bulkany is a major crocodile nest site. Where they get all the eggs from.

Kathy: Bulkany is this big billabong ~ PuleyPuley Dreaming. Where he got lost at MiyerrMiyerr and come back and spewed all the sand from his guts. He went down to salt water, and he got lost. After PuleyPuley took the fire he went down to the salt water. Got lost, and come back. And then he finished up [died] at Bulkany. He spewed all the sand, and he died. Bulkany got a sandy bottom. And the bones are still there, outside on the bank.

Rainbow over Bulkany billabong.

Lily, Bulkany billabong.

Inside the swamp.

Swamps and floating mats: Permanent swamps are the home of dense stands of paperbark trees (*genus Melaleuca*). Floating mats (or floating grass) develop on large permanent bodies of still or slow-moving fresh water. Over 40 plant species contribute to their composition, beginning with aquatics which are 'captured' by rooted vines, and held in place against the banks. Once secured, a range of other plants, including vines, shrubs, trees and ferns establish their niche on the mats. Floating mats are important nesting places for salt water crocodiles and magpie geese.[84]

Paperbark tree.

Linda: That's part of Bynoe Harbour up at the top [top right]. That's where PuleyPuley, the Rainbow Snake, came from. Up through there. The river is the Finniss River. You can see where the Rainbow Snake was twisting and turning.

MiyerrMiyerr (bottom right). That's where the PuleyPuley made his track, all that. When it had the firestick. That's the old river beds going out across the plain, where it lost its mind. He wandered around a lot of the areas of our country, and he finished up at Bulkany.

That's where we used to go and get turtles [below], right down at the end. Near the end of the river.

Nancy: *Muri* tree, it's a *muri*. Fish poison. We take bark and chuck 'im in water, and all the fish come around now. They try to breathe. And they sit on top, you get 'im easy.

Red lilies there.

Fence line, that's Finiss River station.

And there were pigs galore in there.

That's where all the alligators are eating all the bullockies now.

'Fence line, that's Finiss River Station.'

Nancy

Boynoe Harbour; where PuleyPuley, the Rainbow Snake, comes from.

MiyerrMiyerr; where PuleyPuley made his track.

Lotus bird (Jacana jallinacean) catching a dragonfly.

Presence

'All our memories and everything is
from this place ... '
Kim Deveraux

ATTACHMENT AND MEMORY

Kim: This place is like a photo album for us. All our memories and everything is from this place ... [85]

What might it mean to say that your memories are from the land?

Almost everyone will understand the concept and feeling of attachment to place: the sense of love and belonging that links a person to a house, a neighbourhood, a park, a city, a farm. These attachments come into being, reverberate throughout a person's life, and form a spatial and community context for the search for and enjoyment of peacefulness and belonging. Sometimes such attachments become most consciously held when the place is threatened or lost, and many people go to great effort to sustain their attachments to place, and suffer terribly when the places are damaged or destroyed.[86] Indeed, many of the wars of the late twentieth century were about belonging and the struggle to sustain connections between people and place.[87]

Then, too, many people know what it means to have roots: to have ancestors and ancestral places. A great many people alive today are part of one or another of the great diasporas of recent centuries, and people's connections with ancestral places can be reconstructed to show a geography of migration and exile: a psychic terrain of mobility, loss, hope, desperation and arrival. Many Indigenous Australians have also been subjected to dispersal and diaspora; their ancestral connections formed tracks from country to country as colonisation dragged and pushed them here and there across Australia.

Sustained Aboriginal connections to place link attachments, reciprocities, communities and roots. At the heart of these connections is the concept of return. Prior to colonisation, these hunter–gatherer peoples moved from resource site to resource site, from waterhole to waterhole, moving with the seasons, the resources, the Dreaming tracks and the Law. Their movement was always predicated upon their return, and this remains so today.

Like the wet season rains that depart only to return, and like the living things that go up to the high country in the wet season and journey to the floodplains in the dry season, every arrival is a return. The tracks are recursive, and the country holds the signs that are the evidence of those who come and go, and come back again.

Geese in flight.

RETURNS

The necessity of the return pervades Mak Mak culture, and the moral force of the return sustains the kinship and totemic systems, the use and care of place, and the lives and deaths of the people. It forms the common ground between people like April, who were taken or sent away to school, and people like Margy, who grew up in the country. The White-breasted Sea-eagle Dreaming keeps returning in new generations of Mak Mak people and birds. The country keeps returning in the being of the people who take care of it. Not only are people and other living things nurtured so that their lives continue, but as people go about their daily life in the country, the country offers up new people by impelling itself into women [*mirr*] who then give birth. The names of their ancestors cycle out of the ground and through people's lives today. The ancestors' discarded tools lie on the ground to be picked up and used again, and their voices are heard returning on the wind.

Kathy: We hear them. When the wind rustles the leaves, that's the old people talking to us.

Kim Deveraux tells about her life:

Kim: When we were small, when we used to come here [into the homeland], we used to come here for fishing and that, and camping. We used to catch big barra, everything, turtle, and get all the bush turkey out on the plain when it's been burnt. We used to come here with everyone, all my family, and the old people too. They were still alive when I was little. We used to come out here in a big gang. Other times, just come out with my Mum and Dad, or Nana (Nancy), Auntie Margy mob ~ any time ...

... When we was growing up in this country, from little kid time, right up from babies right up till now, we've always spent time in this country, always ... This place is like a photo album for us, you know. All our memories and everything is from this place, from kid time. You know, we never had friends in town because we were always out here. All our family was our friends, my sisters, cousins, whole lot, when we come out here.[88]

Mak Mak people do not mark their presence by enduring monuments; indeed, one could say that the country is their enduring monument.[89] It takes a knowledgeable and discerning eye to see the care, just as it takes a knowledge of history to be able to recognise the traces of past actions, to link those actions with today's actions, and to assert a return.

Stories hold knowledge in place. For example, the legendary figure called PutjuPutju (PurrtyuPurrtyu) travels the land, but has his home in PatjPatj billabong:

[handwritten margin note:] Spending time in the Country in this section gives us more of an insider perspective that doesn't discuss outside the country at all (?)

Linda: The Mak Mak Marranunggu have a Dreamtime navigator: old PurrtyuPurrtyu [PutjuPutju], who lives at a place called PatyPaty [PatjPatj]. PurrtyuPurrtyu is a mythological being who travels in a dugout canoe called a *larrwurr*. To direct his course, PurrtyuPurrtyu uses a long pole made from *mowingy* (ironwood). This wood is poisonous and was used in the old times to make weapons to kill our enemies. Anyway, PurrtyuPurrtyu travels like this: he pushes once, he pushes, twice, and with a third push with his long pole PurrtyuPurrtyu will be wherever PurrtyuPurrtyu wanted to be.[90]

The evidence of former generations of people endures in stories. It is also present physically, in the land. The quarry sites and stone tools, for example, remain as evidence of the lives and actions of the old people. Among the staple foods of the Aboriginal people who lived here in earlier times was rice grass. The technology of processing rice grass involved grinding the grains, so the sites where the grindstones were quarried and kept were central to people's livelihoods. These sites remain significant today as visible links with the ancestors: they connect people across generations, testifying to continuities in place.

Kathy: That's near PatjPatj billabong. There's white quartz rocks there, and jungle there too. Little dry jungles and little quartz ridges up there. All along there there's grinding stones, for rice grass. Dry ridge with jungle, stone tool area.

Nancy with grindstone.
(Photo by D. Rose)

"Reading the landscape"

To look at a place with a knowledgeable eye is to see environmental history, sacred history, disaster, labour, memories, achievements, non-human lives and more. Every 'sight' holds a story. Mak Mak people today hold knowledge from previous generations: for example, where there used to be a little jungle, how it came to be marked by one lone palm tree (*Livistona benthamii*), and when that last palm tree died; or, how the mouth of the river has changed, where the salt water used to meet the fresh water and where it does so today.

Time is thus visible here, not as a geometrical concept, but as place. There is a present time of living things that unfolds in real and located places through real relationships. As well, there is the accumulation of history and memory in place. Place becomes complex in its specific gravity: it is and refers to itself, and it holds and refers to all that has happened there. Its very being, while wondrously dense, is also immensely vulnerable, because the ongoing life of the place happens through the actions and memories of ephemeral living beings.

DEATH AND BEYOND

One of Nancy's fathers was Green Ant Paddy. His name came from Didjini (the Green Ant Dreaming place), and when he was nearing the end of his life he tried to return, so that he could die and be buried in his place:

Kathy: Green Ant Paddy was found by my father at a place near Linda's Yard which is Karkar [in 1958]. He was under a little shelter, a little lean-to, and Dad had pulled up in an old army vehicle and he said to him, 'Old man, you sick?'

And he reckons, 'Yes, old man, I'm going to finish now'. And he said, 'Why don't you go to the hospital?' He reckons, 'No, old man, I'm going back to my country to die'. And the place that he was going to be buried was at Didjini, but he didn't make it, poor bugger.[91]

Kathy: Green ants. One of Mum's fathers' name was Green Ant Paddy. He was buried at Karkar. Old Jarrabak, his name.

Mak Mak people have three main types of ceremony: initiation, secret gendered rituals and funerals. The first two are not suitable for public discussion, but funerals are important public events which involve larger communities of people. Funerals are organised around three moments: the burial, the house-warming and the 'rag burning'. In the burial, the body is buried in accordance with Anglo-Australian law. Once the body is buried, the house-warming ritual enables the living to resume their daily lives. A year or more later, the final ceremony — the rag burning, which is also the most widely attended — is held. This ritual ensures the final departure of the spirit of the deceased.

Rag burning is attended by people who are part of a regional network; they trade with each other, marry each other, sing and dance the same genres, and contribute to each other's ceremonial life. Formerly they fought each other, and recently many of them were involved in the dispute over the land. The guests are all considered to be 'family' within this broader community of kin and countrymen.

Green ants: *Oecophylla smaragdina* work as a team to construct their nests. One encounters them most commonly when one disturbs the nest. They have a powerful bite, but the effects do not linger. They also have the ability to refrain from biting until they have swarmed all over the creature that disturbed them. One is rarely bitten by one ant, usually it is more like 50 or 100 bites, all at once. In some parts of North Australia, green ants figure in Dreaming stories as agents who arouse the dead with their bites. They are used in Indigenous medicine, and can be eaten for a snack.

The more immediate family of the deceased prepares the ceremony ground, and guests contribute fabric that is hung up around the ceremony ground during the ritual. All the goods that the dead person left are gathered together. Many of the items will be put into a hole in the ground to be burnt (hence, 'rag burning'), while valuable items the family will retain are stacked around the hole so that they can be 'smoked' (passed through the smoke). All the relations of the dead person are also smoked, and at the closing the relations are all washed. The deceased's house, car and other possessions are smoked. In the end, the fabric is shared out to all the special guests.

Signs of the ritual remain for years, but eventually they are submerged back into the country. Similarly, people are remembered for years, but in the end they merge into the category of ancestors. They become a presence that remains as a beneficent force; nameless now, they are known to have existed because the country exists.

When Mak Mak people call out to their ancestors for tucker, they call to people who were buried in the area, or who were born in the area:

Kathy: At Karkar we sing out to Jawidjatabak [Green Ant Paddy] because his grave is about a mile away from the river and it's a good fishing spot there and that's where he is, that's where his spirit is. At PatyPaty we'd sing out to our uncle, Uncle Leo, because that's his country, there where he was born.[92]

Generations follow generations, connected not simply by kinship and descent, but by the weaving of people's lives into the land. People today know and visit the same places to do many of the same things that their forebears did. They are connected not just by action, but also by knowledge.

As Kathy says:

Kathy: We've been born in it, we've been handed down tradition from generations. We've got seven [named] generations of Marranunggu people here with us that are the White Eagle side, and the law's been handed down ... and it has never ever been broken.[93]

what does this mean?
Born by blood ties or ties to the land
(both ~?)

Les Waditj burns clothing in a mortuary ritual. (Mak Mak family photo, 1987)

Material hanging from the trees. The material is used to create a ritual enclosure, and after the ritual is finished, it is taken down and distributed by close surviving relatives to the people who have come to assist in the rag burning ceremony. (Mak Mak family photo, 1987)

Nancy Daiyi and Calvin Deveraux at smoking ceremony. (Mak Mak family photo, 1987)

NOMADISM

People often misunderstand the concept of nomadism: a common idea seems to be that nomads are free to wander here and there, as they see fit. Such a view misrepresents nomadism as a form of subsistence activity and as a serious way of life. It would be a rare human society that could afford to wander at will. Societies are territorial, and people's subsistence activities depend on knowledge of the land, the waters, the plants and animals. Their ongoing subsistence further depends on control in one form or another, and these are matters of life and death. For example, one cannot plan to rely on a certain place that is a source of fresh water, only to arrive and find that somebody else has used it all up. Knowledge is held within a system of use and access rights.

For Mak Mak people, a moral human life depends neither on staying in place, nor on wandering at will, but on returning. The traces that remain when the person who made them is gone are both a sign and a promise — they are a sign of their former presence, and a promise of their future return. Living things return, and leave again, crossing time and space. Country holds time and stories together, and every return is a moral action, a promise fulfilled.

Nomadism as a way of life (rather than a post-industrial fantasy) depends on knowledge, and much of this knowledge concerns the communicative web that constitutes country. As April explained in relation to fire, '... country tells you where and when to burn'. And, as Kathy said in reference to the coming of the dry season, ' ... Dragonfly — that tells you big mob fish, barramundi, everything. Fishing time. Start of the Dry, when they come out, dragonfly. You start to get itchy feet yourself. Itchy to go fishing.'

The country is full of messages that call to people. For Mak Mak people, like so many Aboriginal people, nomadism is not a matter of being pushed from place to place as resources become scarce, but rather of being called from place to place as food comes into plenty.

The call of country is sensuous — it communicates by the smell of the rain, the feel of the breeze, the flight of the dragonfly, the sounds of leaves; by the hundred simultaneous events, and by the intervals; by the tracks and by the memories. Country calls on people in the fullness of their being, and so they find their fullness of being in interacting with country. When Mak Mak people try to put into words something of what it means to them to live this connection with Dreamings and place, they say:

> My strength.
> The strength of that land.
> You can feel it in yourself, you belong there.
> It's your country, your dust, your place.
> You remember the old people.
> The white eagles always greet me.
> It's home.
> Safety and security.
> You see the birds, you see the country,
> and your senses come back to you.
> You know what to do and where to go.
> (Mak Mak people)

When Linda calls out to crocs at PatjPatj billabong, she is doing what her uncle used to do. He was named PatjPatj, and the billabong was a significant place for him. This billabong is also one of the main places of Old Man PurrtyuPurrtyu, the Dreamtime navigator. Here he met up with the Dingo who had come from Djulurrk, where the animals had all gathered when Old Man Karramala called them in by blowing his didjeridu across the land.

The moral force of return thus links known generations of people with legendary figures like the Dreamtime navigator, and with the Dreaming tracks and Dreaming figures whose living presence pervades and endures. All this remains in connection because Mak Mak people keep telling the stories and returning.

DANGER

There is danger here. In addition to the crocodiles, and the possibility of dying of thirst in the Dry or drowning in the Wet, there is more. Gendered country constitutes one such danger. Up in the high country one area is for men, and another is for women.

Linda described going across the stony area of men's country:

Linda: Before we go up onto that Tabletop, any of the women, we call out to the country first, and we ask for our grandfather to protect us when we go up there. Whenever we come to any special places we look at the ground and we point our elbow out ... to whatever that place is ... [94]

Similarly, there are places up in the high country that are especially for women, and are particularly associated with the mermaids. These places, and the mermaids themselves, are part of women's secret knowledge (although, of course, the knowledge of their existence is public).

Secret places and secret knowledge are managed through the interplay of public and secret knowledge. People can only know where not to go if they know that the place is forbidden, and people's desire to avoid the forbidden is enhanced by the knowledge that their own understanding is insufficient. They really do not know what they would be fooling around with, but they know that it is dangerous, and that there are severe penalties (both direct and indirect) for error or foolishness.

Along with the danger of gendered places, the country is alive with extraordinary beings. Margy told the story of her encounter with a dingo [the little black dog] who steals people. Like many Mak Mak stories, this is the outside or open layer of a story with many depths.

Margy: There's an old man and his young boy walking around there [near Marenja]. They went hunting and this little boy, he seen this little black dog and that little boy said to his father, 'Daddy, one little puppy dog coming. Can I have him?'

Linda: Looking toward Marenja hills. You're looking across PatjPatj to that big open plain. Marenja is powerful and dangerous too.

He says, 'No, you keep going, boy. Don't! Leave that dog behind.' He kept going and that little dog kept following him and that little dog turned off ~ you know when that grass fold over like a little tunnel, well that little dog disappeared in there and that little boy crawled in after him.

Well, he didn't know, but he got to a big place. He got to a big place and when he stood up, there was this young girl standing there and he said, 'Hey, you have a look this little black puppy dog?'

She reckons, 'No'.

He reckons, 'Yeah, little dog, I've been following little black puppy dog here'.

She reckons, 'Well, I'm that little black puppy dog!', and she closes the hole up, wouldn't let him out ...

... You know, Mum told us that story, and it was handed down to her. Now, over at Param, we went there for turtle, that's on Finniss River station, we went there for turtle, and there's this little black pup. You know, you don't see them very often here, and I chased that little dog. Mum was screaming and swearing at me, said 'Don't you chase that dog.' Anyhow, I kept going, and there was only young saplings then, and I ran through there, and she was still screaming at me, and then when she told me that it'll turn into a man, I come running back out of there. Then she told us this story.

And I said, oh, well, now I have found the connection between this story and when Mum was swearing at me because of that little black dog. Mum was frightened for me.[95]

Pulij is the term for dangerous; it is often translated as 'poison'. Some places are dangerous because they are restricted to particular persons, and other dangerous places make people sick or crippled. One such place is Gubirri, a *pulij* place and a Dreaming place for the Dingo. The Dingo is part of the story for Djulurrk. When Old Man Goose called all the animals in for the ceremony, Dingo came too. He was in the shape of a man, and he was hungry too. He wanted to cook some yams for himself, but the Rainbow Snake had stolen the fire. Dingo was trying to light the fire, but he couldn't get it to light, because the Rainbow Snake had stolen it. He rubbed the firestick until his hands were blistered, and in his frustration he went ahead and ate the yams raw. These were toxic yams, and so they burnt his throat. Away Dingo went, walking and howling, then crawling and howling, from billabong to billabong, until, still howling, he turned into a dingo. The hill where he finished his travels is Gubirri, and it is a dangerous place (see Map of Mak Mak Dreamings, p. xiii).

Kathy: Look at the dingo's eyes (right). Talk about Crawling Man Dreaming? When you look at that dingo, you can tell that story straight away.

They came for ceremony, the whole lot of them, all the animals. And *kenbi* man, Goose, he was the *kenbi* man, didjeridu player.

And PuleyPuley, that's the Rainbow Snake, took the fire away. They couldn't light the fire. He tried to make fire. He couldn't make fire. That dog was rubbing firestick, trying to make fire. You look, the dog [foot] got black black blister.

This one *migut* [Dingo], he got sick of trying to make fire, and he eat the tucker now, whole lot. That's why he been eat it raw one. Cheeky yam [*mimirr*]. When he tasted the cheeky yam, when he ate the tucker, it bit his tongue. That sap is a cheeky one, just like a mustard. You know how that mustard taste? Same like that, cheeky yam, when it's raw one.'

Not only Dingo, but all the animals got their own non-human voices from eating toxic yams.

Migut (*Dingo*).

Kathy: All that fire went away, see, and they couldn't eat that tucker any more because it wasn't cooked, but they were hungry so they ate it, and when they ate that yam, because it's sticky and that sap burned their mouth, they sang out. And when they sang out, they couldn't speak language now. They sang out like Dingo, like, make their own sound, all the animals. 'Wuk Wuk Wuk', like you can hear that bird [owl], and he started turning into Wukwuk [the owl].

Dingo kept crawling, following the billabongs south, and he finished up at Gubirri. That's the Dreaming for that *migut*, that dingo. There's quartz amethyst there, little rocks, sharp pointy ones, that's the dingo's tooth. That shows his tooth, and that's where that Dreaming finished up, and that's why that place is what we call *pulij*: it's a dangerous place.

We're not allowed to climb up or walk around on that hill. We don't hunt in that area between the two hills and gullies. We stay right away from there. We just go right around the outside, because that's a danger place for us.[96]

Gubirri ~ that hill there (top right). He was a man, and he started crawling and howling. He crawled all the way, right up to that Gubirri, and he stopped there.

It's *pulij*: poison country. You might get leprosy there. It's taboo. That's the place now. It's *pulij*. The dust, everything. You can't climb up. You can't eat tucker from there. You can't drink water from there. You don't walk on that hill. One old man was playing cowboy and Indian there, and he ended up with leprosy. He had stumps for hands. No fingers. From playing at Gubirri when he was a young man.

~

Margy: Cheeky yams (bottom right); *mimi* (*Amorphophallus paeoniifolius*). That's not a very big tucker on the end. That's a young one. It grows like a big pumpkin with warts on it. When they mature, towards the Wet, they get a big red flower, and they start giving off a smell like a dead carcass. It attracts blowflies, maybe to pollinate it. The little flies walk all over it. It gives off this awful smell. It's a beautiful flower though.

And the bulb is edible only if you cook it. You can't eat it raw, like in the Dreaming story. You got to check the bulb before you eat it. You break a wart off. We just break it off and test it, rub a finger on it.

You break it off, and you press your thumb against where you broke that piece off, and it's sticky. If there's glitter in the sap it's not ready to eat. It's still cheeky. It burns your mouth. If it is ready, you still have to cook it. You just cook it one time in the ground. Roast it in the ground, and it comes out yellow like pumpkin. Really nice smell. Golden yellow, rich yellow, like pumpkin.

Gubirri hill, Migut (*Dingo*) *Dreaming.*

Mimirr (*'cheeky' yam*).

Migut (*Dingo*), *Crawling Man Dreaming.*

Kathy: That's where old man PutjuPutju met up with this Dingo.

Kathy: And he left quartz crystal behind from his teeth (left).

That's the place: PatjPatj (above). That's where old man PutjuPutju met up with this Dingo here.

That's for old PutjuPutju. That old Dreaming man, eh. From PatjPatj.

Look at his eye, look at his eye. He looks like that old man.

The Dingo walked back and forth between the twin hills of Gubirri and the billabong called PatjPatj. Down at the billabong he met up with the Dreamtime navigator who went around stealing other men's wives, Old PutjuPutju.

Quartz crystal, Migut (Dingo) teeth.

This billabong is covered with patches of floating grass, and there's a story here too. One of the old-time Mak Mak men, Nancy's father's brother, Old Wigma, was lucky enough to catch a mermaid. He was in the high country, where the mermaids live in the fresh flowing spring water, and he managed to sneak up on her and grab her by her long hair. He wrapped the hair around his wrists so that she couldn't get away, and he took her away from her own people and brought her to live with him, and he cut her long hair and made a belt out of it. One day, though, when she went to PatjPatj to get water, she saw a hole in the floating grass and she dived right in. 'See you later, I'm going home,' she called, and she was gone.

MERMAIDS

The annual journey from the high country in the wet season to the floodplains in the Dry necessitates a return to the high country in the next wet season.

Margy: Nguntjurr we call it. Wangi Falls in Litchfield National Park. It was a big women's ceremony place here. And Mum was the last Marranunggu woman to have ceremony here.

Linda: This is hill country. Tabletop Range on top, where the spring country starts up: Nguntjurr and Makanba.

All this Tabletop country, this Litchfield Park is mermaid. Mermaid, right through this Tabletop country, mermaids.

We call that mermaid *pegu yanginmarra*. She has got a tail like a yabbie [crawfish].

Nancy: Young girls dance, where you splash the water. All get in a circle and splash the water. They sing that mermaid song ~ *mamakiki*.

High country where Old Wigma grabbed the mermaid.

Marranunggu and Marrithiel men involved in a rag burning ceremony at Meneling near Batchelor, possibly 1950s. Left to right: George Wigma, Robert Maramir, Tyirrepit, Frankie Dunmir, Leo Djakaboi, Peter Melyen and Captain Atie. (Mak Mak family photo)

Old Wigma went to the high country to grab the mermaid because this is where they live: in the flowing spring water of the ranges. These high country spring waters are gendered and sacred, dangerous to those who do not belong there. April's *mirr* is connected with mermaids, and when she describes Makanba, a high country spring-fed creek system, she is speaking of her birth place as well as a place that is home to the mermaids with whom she is connected:

April: This place, white man way they call it Bamboo Creek, we call it Makanba, and this place here got lot of Dreaming. This place is one of the heart places for our people. This place, ceremonies been here, old time, even when I was a little girl, used to be big mob dancing here, corroboree.[97]

One of the main mermaid places used to be Nguntjurr — Wangi Falls (see maps, pp. xi and xiii). This was a place specifically for women's ritual, when young women were initiated into adulthood, and were brought into the water to meet the mermaids. And although the specific initiation rituals have not been performed for many years, Mak Mak women continue to communicate with mermaids.

Nguntjurr (*Wangai Falls*), mermaid place.

Today Wangi Falls is one of the most popular tourist destinations in the whole Park. It can be dangerous, and many Aboriginal people in the region attribute the large number of tourist deaths there to the fact that this is a sacred and dangerous place. Mak Mak people feel the impact of tourism as estrangement. They really only want to go there when it is not crowded with strangers, and, as a consequence, they go there less and less:

Nancy: Oh Nguntjurr, 'im poorfella. Oh, it make me sorry that country, I tell you. You know why? Because of the mermaids. No more *yanginmarra* [mermaids] there now, might be finished. All gone, all scattered.

I heard mermaids when I was at Makanba.

Kathy: You hear them?

Nancy: Like a Torres Strait Island pigeon [a soft cooing sound]. When daylight come they got to go back home.

Might be they're not there at Nguntjurr any more. Because there's too many people go there.

I was worried, you know, I been start crying. This place should be for young women, for mermaids, this place here is the main one. And mermaids supposed to be here, but they all along the little creeks now.

Kathy: The mermaids should be here, but they're crying because too many people go there. Mum says they should be making their noise there at the sandbar. Mum taught us to pound the water, make that drum sound.

They should be making that sound on the sandbar that's in the middle of the pool there.

I don't know what's happened now. They might be afraid to come back because of the house there, that kiosk. They might be further into the spring country, down towards Makanba way.

Nancy: All the little springs, they walk around there, I reckon.

Kathy: Like all the rest of the other native animals, they go long way [far away] because there's too much tourist. You find them in funny places, now, all that kangaroo, rock wallaby, they're all in funny places, they're getting pushed out from their own homes.

Nguntjurr (*Wangai Falls*), *mermaid place — sacred and dangerous.*

Margy: Bloody tourists in there. Mermaids not playing there now that whitefellas taking over.

Linda: All the mermaids like to be in that place [left]: clean water and sandy ground. Mermaids love these little falls, they let their hair flow in the water.

Kathy: Makanba. Mum was camped over here for two weeks, and she could hear the mermaids singing out, because they were making their way back up the stream. She could hear them moving at night. Singing. And she was saying they were getting distressed because they were getting pushed out of their homes, out of their natural environment. Because of tourism and that sort of thing.

Contemporary globalised nomadism brings strangers into places as tourists. For most, their travel is a series of intensely experienced but short-term visits with no real intention of return. I keep thinking that global nomadism is marginalising, and could even destroy, the contemporary Mak Mak nomadism of returns and connection. Mak Mak people think about these things too:

April: Well, us Mak Mak Marranunggu, we following old people, and we'll follow them, and we mightn't die physically, but we'll die in our heart if we lose this country.[98]

Makanba — where the mermaids let their hair flow in the water [left].

I have been awe-struck by the resilience of Mak Mak people as they manage one crisis event after another. Their strength, as they repeatedly say, comes from their country and their connections. As a privileged guest, I have been shown how people find and exercise their strength, and in this book we have sought to share that knowledge with you, the reader.

Mak Mak strength grows out of knowledge, and that knowledge is embedded in place. It follows that Mak Mak knowledge invites us to open our hearts to the many living things whose tracks cross a given place, and to the richness of time as it binds life into country. As well, it asks us to find ways to interact with non-humans, and thus to enlarge our concept of sentience.

Mak Mak knowledge demands that we think about love in relation to place. For the future of places, and the future of the world, can love of place shimmer in the very heart of our lives?

Linda and her daughter Chloe, at Makanba.

ABOUT THE CONTRIBUTORS

Nancy Daiyi was born and educated in Mak Mak country. She was the senior surviving member of the clan, and thus was the elder, which is to say, the teacher, the authority and the role model. Her bi-cultural skills and life history imbued her with strength, courage, and determination. These are all qualities which she passed on to her children and grandchildren.

April Bright was born at Makanba in the hill country. She endured separation from her family and country under government regulations that prescribed the removal of 'part-Aboriginal' children from their families. She divides her time between her homeland and the city (Darwin). In Darwin, having worked for years in the field of Aboriginal medicine, she is now retired.

Kathy Deveraux was born in Mak Mak country and was educated in Anglo-Australian schools as well as in the bush. She now divides her time between MakMak country and her work the town of Batchelor where she teaches at Batchelor Institute of Indigenous Tertiary Education.

Margaret Daiyi was born in Mak Mak country and educated in the bush as well as in Anglo-Australian schools. She has taken on major responsibilities for cattle and for mimosa control in the homelands. A superb hunter (*milijin*), she works daily to sustain Mak Mak country. For a number of years after this book was first published she served as a regional representative to the Northern Land Council and was further elected to the Executive.

Richard Daiyi was born in Mak Mak country and educated in the bush as well as in Anglo-Australian schools. He has held numerous working positions over the years, and now works in the field of Aboriginal health.

Linda Ford was born in Mak Mak country and educated in the bush as well as in Anglo-Australian schools. She divides her time between her homeland and her position as lecturer at the University of Queensland in Brisbane. She holds a PhD in early childhood education from Deakin University in Australia. She serves on the Council of the Australian Institute of Aboriginal and Torres Strait Islander Studies (see: http://www.aiatsis.gov.au/corporate/council members.html).

Deborah Rose is Professor of Social Inclusion at Macquarie University, Sydney. She has worked in the arena of land rights as the anthropologist for claimant groups and as consulting anthropologist for the Aboriginal Land Commissioner. Her work is interdisciplinary and is focussed on social and ecological justice. More information can be found at http://www.ecological humanities.org/rose.html.

Sharon D'Amico is a Seattle, USA based photographer specialising in nature, travel and cultures. Informed by her first career as a science teacher, she incorporates an understanding of nature and the environment into her images of the natural world. Three decades of environmental and social justice activism coupled with a fascination with different cultures has led her to photograph people and places on five continents. Her work has appeared in publications throughout the world and can be found at www.damicophotography.com.

ABOUT THE CHILDREN

Calvin Deveraux was a child when the work leading to this book began. He now heads the cattle business at Twin Hills, the commercial arm of the Mak Mak White Eagle Association. He too has served as a representative to the Northern Land Council. **Bill** (a young man at the time we wrote the book) works with earthmoving equipment and does erosion control for Twin Hills, **Rankin** does contract work in the cattle industry including at Twin Hills, while **Gary** is studying to become a policeman and **Kim** is raising a family. **Chloe Ford** (p. 151) is completing high school in Brisbane. Her younger sister **Emily** regrets not having been born in time to be part of the book. She is agitating for a follow-up book on 'the new generation of leaders'.

ABOUT THE CLAN
(See clan photo, pp. vii and 98)

The Mak Mak clan is a far flung group of people, all of whom are descended from an ancestral couple Taybut and Ngulikan. The branches of the family that now identify as Mak Mak Marranunggu are the descendants of this couple through their son Kuwatjangu. He had four sons and a daughter. The sons were Wemen, Wigma, Tjarrabak, and Djakaboi. The daughter was Mangilimba. The children of the four men are classed as brothers and sisters. They include the child of Wemen, Elsie Goyda, and the children of Tjarrabak, who include Kapa, Wadjit and Peter Melyen. Elsie Goyda's descendants include Billy Liddy and his children. Kapa's descendants include Henry Moreen and his children. Wadjit's children include Frank Spry, Besie Copeland, and Ruby Zimmerman. Peter Melyen's descendants include Brian Melyen and his children.

Djakaboi's children from his first wife were Peter Melyen, Bilawuk, Fred Waditj, Pandela, and Alice Goyder. From his second wife his children were Leo Djakaboi (Patj Patj), and Nancy Daiyi. Yilngi is Nancy's sister; they have the same mother but different fathers.

Bilawuk's children include Pavalina Nickaloff, and Majeta (Kolya), along with several deceased children. Pavalina's children include Richard, Michelle, Peter, Paul, Luanna. Their children are members or affiliates of the clan.

Another set of Bilawuk's children includes Ann Majar, Daisy Majar, Audrey Majar, Mindy Majar, Jane Majar, and Karen Majar. These women and their children identify strictly with their father's clan.

Fred Waditj was another of Djakaboi's children. His children are John, Leslie, Sandra, Laurie, and Jeffrey (deceased). Their children include Sandra's children David, Sean, Rory and Andrew, and Laurie's children Ngalierra and Ngamuk.

Pandela was another of Djakaboi's children. Her child is April Bright, and April's children include Annie, Errol and Shane. April's grandchildren include Shari, Robert, Ashley, Kylie, Chrisiny, Ebony, Shanai and Shane.

Alice Goyder was another of Djakaboi's children. Her daughter is Miriam Raymond.

Leo Djakaboi (Patj Patj) had one son, Andrew Belyuen.

(Left to right, standing) Waditj, Nancy, Anju, Bilawuk, Goyder,
Wigma and T. Nickaloff; (children in front) Rose and Pavalina.
(Mak Mak family photo)

Nancy Daiyi has four children, Kathy, Margaret, Richard, and Linda. Kathy's children are Donna, Kim, Rankin, and Gary. Margaret's children are Calvin and Billy. Richard's children are Cherise, Richard, Helen, Karina and Henry. Linda's children are Chloe and Emily.

Yilngi had four children: Douglas Atie, Tracey Atie, Theresa Atie, and Patrick Atie. Tracy's children are David and John. Theresa's child is Amelia Rose.

NOTES

1. K. Deveraux, 'Looking at country from the heart', in D. Rose and A. Clarke (eds), *Tracking Knowledge in North Australian Landscapes; Studies in Indigenous and Settler Ecological Knowledge Systems*, Darwin: North Australia Research Unit, 1998, pp. 68–81.

2. C. Dunlop and L. Webb, 'Flora and vegetation', in C. Haynes, M. Ridpath and M. Williams (eds), *Monsoonal Australia; Landscape, Ecology and Man in the Northern Lowlands*, Rotterdam: A. Balkema, 1991, pp. 41–60.

3. A good introduction to the didjeridu in the musical genre of the Wagait region is the compact disc recording *Bunggridj-bunggridj: Wangga Songs by Alan Maralung, North Australia*, International Institute for Traditional Music, Smithsonian Folkways, Washington DC: Smithsonian Institution, 1993.

4. D. Horton (ed), *The Encyclopaedia of Aboriginal Australia: Aboriginal and Torres Strait Islander history, society and culture*, Canberra: Aboriginal Studies Press, 1994.

5. J. Brock, *Top End Native Plants*, Darwin, NT: John Brock, 1988.

6. K. Deveraux, op. cit., 1998, p. 72 (emphasis in original).

7. The term comes from E. Levinas, in S. Hand (ed), *The Levinas Reader*, Oxford: Basil Blackwell Ltd, 1989, p. 210. See also D. Rose, *Nourishing Terrains; Australian Aboriginal Views of Landscape and Wilderness*, Canberra: Australian Heritage Commission, 1996.

8. Transcript of Maranunga [Marranunggu] Proceedings, October 1993, Special Hearing before the Wagait Traditional Ownership Dispute Committee, p. 395.

9. H. Lewis, 'Traditional ecological knowledge — some definitions', in N. Williams and G. Baines (eds), *Traditional Ecological Knowledge*, ANU, Canberra: Centre for Resource and Environmental Studies, 1993, pp. 8–12. See also D. Rose (ed), *Country in Flames; Proceedings of the 1994 Symposium on Biodiversity and Fire in North Australia*, The Australian National University, Canberra and Darwin: Biodiversity Unit, Department of the Environment, Sport and Territories and the North Australia Research Unit, 1995.

10. D. Bowman, 'Tansley Review No. 101: The impact of Aboriginal landscape burning on the Australian biota', *New Phytologist*, 1998, 140, pp. 385–410. See also D. Rose, op. cit., 1996.

11. L. Head, 'Landscapes socialised by fire: Post contact changes in Aboriginal fire use in northern Australia, and implications for prehistory', *Archaeology in Oceania*, 1994, 29, pp. 172–181.

12. A. Bright, 'Burn grass' in D. Rose (ed), op. cit., 1995, pp. 59–62.

13. ibid. See also B. Adam, 'Running out of time: Global crisis and human engagement', in M. Redclift and T. Benton (eds), *Social Theory and the Global Environment*, London: Routledge, 1994.

14. Transcript of Maranunga Proceedings, op. cit., 1993, p. 350.

15. R. Braithewaite and J. Estbergs, 'Firebirds of the Top End', *Australian Natural History*, 1988, 22, 7, pp. 298–302.

16. D. Bowman, op. cit., 1998.

17. Transcript of Maranunga Proceedings, op. cit., 1993, pp. 293–294.

18. Transcript of Maranunga Proceedings, op. cit., 1993, pp. 297–298.

19. G. Webb, 'The influence of season on Australian crocodiles', in C. Haynes, M. Ridpath and M. Williams (eds), *Monsoonal Australia; Landscape, Ecology and Man in the Northern Lowlands*, Rotterdam: A. Balkema, 1991, pp. 125–131.

20. D. Rose, L. Ford, and N. Daiyi, 'The Way We Are (Working in Flux)', in E. Greenwood, K. Neumann and A. Sartori (eds), *Work in Flux*, pp. 10–19, Melbourne: The University of Melbourne History Department, 1995, p. 15.

21. K. Deveraux, op. cit, 1998, pp. 74, 72.

22. ibid., p. 77.

23. ibid., p. 73.

24. E. Povinelli, *Labor's Lot; The Power, History and Culture of Aboriginal Action*, Chicago: University of Chicago Press, 1993, p. 139.

25. H. Arendt, *Between Past and Future; Six Exercises in Political Thought*, London: Faber and Faber, 1954 [1961].

26. J. Ring, *The Political Consequences of Thinking; Gender and Judaism in the Work of Hannah Arendt*, Albany: State University of New York Press, 1997.

27. H. Arendt, op. cit., 1954 [1961], p. 42.

28. A number of contemporary scholars argue that western notions of time are not actually reducible to circles and lines, that these geometric structures seek to over-simplify, and that increasingly it is clear that simplifying important matters such as time does more harm than good. Many western authors also discuss the rhythmic qualities of the natural world (for example, see B. Adam, op. cit., 1994).

29. A. Bright, op. cit, 1995, pp. 60–61.

30. P. Hadlington and J. Johnston, *An Introduction to Australian Insects*, Sydney: New South Wales University Press, 1982.

31. A. Anderson and R. Baithwaite, 'Plant-animal interactions', in C. Finlayson and I. Oertzen (eds), *Landscape and Vegetation Ecology of the Kakadu Region, Northern Australia*, Dordrecht (Netherlands): Kluwer Academic Publishers, 1996, pp. 137–154.

32. K. Deveraux, op. cit., 1998, p. 74.

33. ibid.

34. Transcript of Maranunga Proceedings, op. cit., 1993, p. 749.

35. K. Deveraux, op. cit., 1998, p. 73.

36. Transcript of Maranunga Proceedings, op. cit., 1993, p. 752.

37. P. Palmer and A. Arthington, *The Barramundi, Lates calcarifer (Bloch) — A Review of Biology and Ecology with Particular Reference to Australia*, AES Monograph 1/86, Brisbane: Griffith University, 1986.

38. Peter Latz makes this perspicacious point in 'Fire in the Desert: Increasing biodiversity in the short term, decreasing it in the long term', in D. Rose (ed), *Country in Flames; Proceedings of the 1994 Symposium on Biodiversity and Fire in North Australia*, The Australian National University, Canberra and Darwin: Biodiversity Unit, Department of the Environment, Sport and Territories and the North Australia Research Unit, 1995, pp. 77–86.

39. K. Deveraux, op. cit., 1998, p. 73.

40. H. Thompson and D. Goodfellow, *Common Birds of the Darwin Area*, Winnellie, NT: Sandpiper Productions, 1987.

41. Transcript of Maranunga Proceedings, op. cit., 1993, p. 406.

42. H. Cogger, *Reptiles and Amphibians of Australia*, Sydney: A. H. & A.W. Reed Pty Ltd, 1975.

43. A. Bright, op. cit., 1995, p. 62.

44. D. Rose, L. Ford and N. Daiyi, op. cit, 1995, p. 14.

45. Transcript of Maranunga Proceedings, op. cit., 1993, pp. 412–413.

46. H. Thompson and D. Goodfellow, op. cit., 1987; G. Miles, *Wildlife of Kakadu & the Top End of the Northern Territory, Australia*, Alice Springs: Barker Souvenirs, 1988.

47. Transcript of Maranunga Proceedings, op. cit., 1993, p. 357.

48. D. Rose, L. Ford and N. Daiyi, op. cit, 1995, p. 14.

49. K. Deveraux, op. cit., 1998, p. 76.
50. L. Corbett, *The Dingo in Australia and Asia*, Sydney: University of New South Wales Press, 1995.
51. The date of 4000 BP (Before the Present) was kindly provided by Darryl Guse, and is based on his research at the nearby Reynolds River. Other information in this paragraph is summarised from J. Chappell, 'Contrasting Holocene sedimentary geologies of lower Daly River, northern Australia, and lower Sepik-Ramu, Papua New Guinea', *Sedimentary Geology*, 1993, 83, pp. 339–358.
52. To the best of my knowledge, the term 'cultural cleansing' was first used in an analysis of frontier colonisation by E. Furniss, *The Burden of History; Colonialism and the Frontier Myth in a Rural Canadian Community*, Vancouver: UBC Press, 1999, p. 42.
53. Australian Bureau of Statistics, <http://www.abs.gov.au/> (viewed March 2011).
54. In 1953, government officials talked about revoking the reserve so as to make it more accessible to white pastoralists, but in the end the area was reduced rather than revoked, and a smaller reserve remained; according to Correspondence contained in the Australian Archives ACT Regional Office, Series A 452/1, Item 1953/39.
55. Transcript of Maranunga Proceedings, op. cit., 1993, p. 422.
56. Intercultural relations in these densely conflicted frontier zones were complex in the extreme. See for example, W. Stanner, 'Durmugam: A Nangiomeri', in *White Man Got No Dreaming; Essays 1938–73*, Canberra: Australian National University Press, 1979, pp. 67–105; and D. Rose, 'Signs of life on a barbarous frontier: Intercultural encounters in North Australia', *Humanities Research*, 1998, 2, pp. 17–36.
57. *Bringing them Home, National Inquiry into the Separation of Aboriginal and Torres Strait Islander Children from their Families*, Sydney: Human Rights and Equal Opportunity Commission, 1997.
58. Transcript of Maranunga Proceedings, op. cit., 1993, pp. 324–325.
59. D. Rose, L. Ford and N. Daiyi, op. cit, 1995, p. 16.
60. Transcript of Maranunga Proceedings, op. cit., 1993, p. 387.
61. ibid., p. 395.
62. Majar, Daisy on behalf of herself and on behalf of others of the Werat Clan and Margaret Daiyi on behalf of herself and on behalf of others of the Marranunggu Clan *And* The Northern Land Council; Federal Court of Australia, Olney J. presiding. 1991 decision.
63. K. Deveraux, op. cit., 1998, p. 76.
64. Transcript of Maranunga Proceedings, op. cit., 1993, pp. 307–308.
65. *The Cattle Industry in the Northern Territory*, A Department of the Interior Publication.
66. M. Ridpath, 'Feral mammals and their environments', in C. Haynes, M. Ridpath and M. Williams (eds), *Monsoonal Australia; Landscape, Ecology and Man in the Northern Lowlands*, pp. 169–191, Rotterdam: A. Balkema, 1991, pp. 176–177.
67. M. Considine, 'Buffalo in the Top End', *Ecos*, 1985, 44, pp. 3–12, at p. 4.
68. Personal communication from Jeremy Russell-Smith, 1993.
69. Compaction, like most of these processes, is part of floodplain ecology even without the intervention of buffalo.
70. M.Considine, op. cit., 1985, p. 5.
71. M. Ridpath, op. cit., 1991, p. 183.
72. P. Fogarty, *A Preliminary Survey of Environmental Damage Associated with Activity of Feral Buffalo*, Darwin: Conservation Commission of the Northern Territory, 1982, p. 18.
73. M. Ridpath, op. cit., 1991, p. 184.
74. ibid., pp. 182, 184.

75. J. Russell-Smith and D. Bowman, 'Conservation of monsoon rainforest isolates in the Northern Territory, Australia', *Biological Conservation*, 1992, 59, pp. 51–63.

76. Transcript of Maranunga Proceedings, op. cit., 1993, p. 362 and elsewhere.

77. G. Stoneham and J. Johnston, *The Australian Brucellosis and Tuberculosis Eradication Campaign*, Bureau of Agricultural Economics, Occasional Paper 97, Canberra: Australian Government Publishing Service, 1987.

78. M. Ridpath, op. cit., 1991, pp. 174–175.

79. ibid., pp. 176–179.

80. ibid., p. 185.

81. Transcript of Maranunga Proceedings, op. cit., 1993, p. 315.

82. I. Cowie, 'Weed ecology', in C. Finlayson and I. Oertzen (eds), *Landscape and Vegetation Ecology of the Kakadu Region, Northern Australia*, Dordrecht (Netherlands): Kluwer Academic Publishers, 1996, pp. 113–135.

83. Transcript of Maranunga Proceedings, op. cit., 1993, pp. 310–311.

84. Dunlop and Webb, op. cit., 1991; M. Ridpath, op. cit., 1991.

85. Transcript of Maranunga Proceedings, op. cit., 1993, pp. 403–404.

86. P. Read, *Returning to Nothing; The Meaning of Lost Places*, Cambridge: Cambridge University Press, 1996.

87. M. Ignatieff, *Blood and Belonging: Journeys into the New Nationalism*, New York: Farrar, Straus & Giroux, 1994; D. Curtin, 'Making Peace with the Earth: Indigenous agriculture and the Green Revolution', *Environmental Ethics*, 17, 1995, pp. 59–73.

88. Transcript of Maranunga Proceedings, op. cit., 1993, pp. 403–404.

89. T. Ingold, 'Territoriality and tenure: The appropriation of space in hunting and gathering societies', in *The Appropriation of Nature, Essays on Human Ecology and Social Relations*, Manchester: Manchester University Press, 1986, pp. 130–164.

90. D. Rose, L. Ford and N. Daiyi, op. cit, 1995, p. 19.

91. Transcript of Maranunga Proceedings, February 1994, Special Hearing before the Wagait Traditional Ownership Dispute Committee, p. 702.

92. ibid., p. 751.

93. Transcript of Maranunga Proceedings, op. cit., 1993, p. 290.

94. ibid., p. 351.

95. ibid., p. 419.

96. ibid., p. 350.

97. ibid., p. 324.

98. ibid., p. 357.

INDEX